Diary of a MaD Househusband

Diary of a MaD Househusband

Joseph Oberle

Musings on
life as a
stay-at-home
dad

Kimm Publishing, Inc.
Fridley, Minnesota

Printed in the United States of America.

A 0 9 8 7 6 5 4 3 2 1

Published by Kimm Publishing, Inc., P.O. Box 32927, Fridley, MN 55432-0927

cover design and page design by Scott Kneeskern of kdk DESIGN
cover illustration by Joe Nordstrom

Printed by Kimm Printing, 428 Washington Ave. N., Minneapolis, MN 55401

Library of Congress Catalog Card Number 96-75064

Publisher's Cataloging in Publication
(Prepared by Quality Books Inc.)

Oberle, Joseph.
Diary of a mad househusband : musings on life as a stay-at-home dad / by Joseph Oberle.
p. cm.
ISBN 0-9650741-3-7

1. Househusbands–Humor. 2. Parent and child–Humor. I. Title.

HQ756.6.034 1996 640'.92
QBI96-20038

To my parents, Mary Ann and Tony O, who went through all this years ago but never felt compelled to write a book about it.

Acknowledgments

In putting together this book, I received encouragement and generous help from many people, and I would like to acknowledge their contributions with gratitude:

to Lora, my wife, for giving me the opportunity to experience this great side of fatherhood and for her talent and persistence in editing my manuscript into an interesting form;

to Leo Polack for his patience and generosity in taking on this project;

to Greg Polack and Sherry Tollefson for their time, effort, and hard work in seeing the book through to print;

to Scott Kneeskern for his great ideas, hustle, and extra effort in designing the book, and Brendan Finnegan for his timely assistance in laying it out;

to Joe Nordstrom for his great cover illustration;

to my daughters, Tessa and Paige, for their constant love despite the hours I spend at work and away from them;

and finally, to Seth, the inspiration for this book and the occasional object of my sense of humor. I hope that when he reads this book someday, he feels the love and joy that Lora and I felt in creating it.

Contents

Introduction

It was July 4 when the revolution began at our house – I quit my job as a reporter for a weekly newspaper in Minneapolis and came home to be a househusband and caregiver for my then-sixteen-month-old son, Seth. What I thought was going to be my first day of independence was really my last day of freedom.

My wife, Lora, and I had agreed to undertake this grand experiment in parenting, in which I would be the full-time stay-at-home father and homemaker, of sorts, while she would continue to work, bringing home the bacon necessary to keep our small household functioning. A role reversal like that sounds laudable when you read about it in the newspaper, but it's somewhat daunting when you try it yourself.

This book tells the story of that experiment – how a sports-loving, red-blooded American guy adapted to changing diapers ten times a day, kissing owies, picking up legions of toy cars and blocks, soothing his wife's fragile mother-ego, and cooking broccoli at every other meal. It's been an incredible test of my creativity, a battle of wills where the mighty doesn't always win, and more than anything, a transformation for myself and my family that surprised us at every turn.

For me, it's true that I was no longer reporting to the office to extinguish the deadline fires burning beneath my editor's desk. Instead, I jumped to the call of a busy toddler, whose demands grew with his awareness of all the things in the world that can be demanded. As a reporter, I was chained to my computer and phone by the need to get a story out – at home, I was tethered to my son, whose constant (and sometimes precarious) tearing about the house has sapped the energy out of my thirtysomething-plus body.

Lora and I put a lot of thought into our lifestyle-change. Frustrated with missing most of Seth's waking hours and exhausted from every virus he brought home from day care, we wanted to be raising our child ourselves. For six months prior to this July day, we labored over the decision, arguing back and forth over how it could best be done. The final result was me, sitting on the patio on the Fourth of July, unemployed.

When looked at objectively, the decision seemed obvious, although that didn't make it any easier. One of us had a job with good pay, adequate benefits, excellent security, and the esteem of their employer – and one of us didn't. Unfortunately, I was the odd parent out.

As much as we both wanted Lora to be a stay-at-home mom, our financial situation would not allow it and we were cast into the unknown chasm of Mister Momdom. I reluctantly traded in my reporters notebook for diaper wipes, my pencil for a crayon, and my connections at City Hall for the company of Bert and Ernie, Cookie Monster, and Big Bird.

At the time, we thought that I could use my newfound free time to work at home, writing freelance magazine and newspaper articles. (In my *spare* spare time, I even planned on writing that great American novel I've long talked about.) Of course, that was only the first of many misperceptions we had about househusbandry. This book is filled with the rest.

If the story occasionally seems to report stereotyped relations between men and women, well, it wasn't supposed to be like that. But what I wrote here is what really happened – stereotypical behavior is what I found. Lora and I were both surprised at the feelings that other people expressed and that we ourselves had. It seems that the world is about as ready for househusbands as men are ready to become them.

While this opportunity has seemed like a great gift most of the time, there are times when it's been more of a trial. I always thought that I would love being a parent, but I never imagined that it would be such a thoroughly, constantly draining experience. I couldn't avoid the loudest of tantrums, the dirtiest of diapers, the most nasal of tired-kid whines. I argued about naptimes, agonized over tumbles on the driveway, and locked horns with a stubborn little person about a third of my size. Sometimes, I admit, I even thought of this book as my revenge – it'll embarrass the heck out of Seth someday.

I also found that being a househusband means more than just being a Mister Mom. Physically unequipped to become a housewife, I still acquired the traditional jobs of one and found myself immersed in a lifestyle that revolved around vacuum cleaner bags, dishwasher detergent, and furniture polish. Househusbandry put a new spin on my relationships with my friends, family, and even my own psyche – all of which confronted me with a lot of questions and confusion.

But most importantly, by being a househusband I learned a lot about my son, my wife, and myself. Over the time I was home, Seth and I developed a bond that I will always treasure, Lora and I got to see another side of each other, and I started strangely and inexplicably turning into my own mom – yelling about scattered dirty laundry and nobody wiping their feet when they came in the house.

By treating the madness I experienced with a little humor, I had fun, and I hope the reader will enjoy my experiences, as well – and maybe even glean some insight into the parent/child relationship. This book does not tell you how to be a good househusband – my advice to other husbands who want to try it is the customary "Don't try this at home, I'm a professional." (If this book sells, that is.) But if you must, it's one heck of a ride.

I do recommend this book for nightly reading (for moms as well as dads), a stress-reliever for those ten minutes between when the kids finally fall asleep and you yourself close your eyes in exhaustion. Knowing that someone else is suffering a similar or worse fate is great comfort – doesn't every parent you know talk more about their kids than about what happens at work?

Introduction

This book is not a typical day-by-day diary because the days all seemed to run together. (Feeding and changing a kid is a self-perpetuating cycle that can seem unending.) Besides, it took me weeks to write each entry, squeezing in a few precious minutes during naps and at night, when my wife came home from work.

When Lora came home, I temporarily transformed from Mister Mom back to Mister Dad, but things still stayed basically the same – except that I used a deeper voice when I scolded our kid. I wanted to maintain some kind of role identity, after all.

Either way, I barrelled into parenting full-force, all day and all night long. Becoming a househusband – as you will find – is entering a whole new world.

Part I
Summer

The most important thing you will ever do is to raise your children."
– Former First Lady Barbara Bush speaking at the Wellesley College commencement on June 1, 1990

"Anyone who is driven nuts by children can't be all bad."
– with apologies to W.C. Fields

Chapter 1
Trading Places

What have I got to complain about? So I'm no longer employed as a reporter, a position I worked for years to attain. So I've given up a weekly byline in a competitive publishing market to play house with my son. Is that all bad? It's July, the temperature is eighty degrees with enough breeze to jostle the wind chimes hanging from the back of my house, and I'm sitting on the patio, drinking a glass of ice-cold lemonade and watching my sixteen-month-old son, Seth, chase a plastic ball around the yard.

I guess it's not so bad. Seth is beginning to talk, which provides a little entertainment, and he's developing a pretty good cut at the ball – inspiring dreams of his future glory on the ball field. Only his occasional whine or urgent tug on my sleeve reminds me of my former editors.

It's my first week of being a stay-at-home dad, and I'm slowly adjusting to the role of househusband – so far, I think I can handle it. I gladly respond to Seth's requests because I know the piece of cheese I get for him is going to be good enough and the glass of water will not be dropped back in my lap with demands to add more quotes. Seth knows what he wants when he sends me on assignment, and for at least another six months, until he hits the terrible twos, I expect that he will be satisfied enough with the results to run with them.

I'll admit that I've got my fears about leaving my job. I worry that being out of print will be a threat to my writing career, that my skills will atrophy, that I'll miss adult companionship. But when I recall sixty-hour workweeks (for minimal pay), I quickly justify taking a break. Besides, I plan on working freelance, actually writing what I want to. And with the local newspaper at my feet and CNN just a channel-scan away, I won't lose touch with events outside my backyard. For the first time in years, I don't hear a phone ringing. Yes, my old life is beginning to melt away in the afternoon sun.

Suddenly, Seth is bored with smacking the ball around. He comes and hangs on my knee and whines "unnhh." I guess that means it's time to go to the park.

We jump in the car for our first real trip away from home as Mister Mom and Master Son. A few blocks away, we find Commons Park, not far from the local high school. Within the park is a metal forest of slides and swings and crawling apparati, all suspiciously empty at two-thirty on a Tuesday afternoon. I suddenly feel like I'm playing hookey.

We try a slide, but Seth is a bit too young to handle it on his own and he squirms ferociously when I try to place him at the top. Instead, he sits on the ground near the bottom and begins digging happily in the sand and pebbles – a new experience for him. I sit down and do the same and for a moment am returned to my childhood days of backyard sandcastles besieged by Matchbox cars and armymen. I sift the sand through my fingers nostalgically, and then reach up to scratch my itchy nose. The stench of cigarette butts and cat feces is overwhelming. I jump to my feet, grab Seth and quickly brush off his fingers, which were surely headed for his mouth.

Figuring that the swings would keep Seth from digging in this neighborhood catbox, I head him in that direction. A mother and her son had arrived and were swinging on one of the swings. I put Seth in another and wonder what to say, nervous as a person on the first day of a new job – and a minority to boot.

"Ready, Seth?" I ask, rhetorically. "Here we go."

"Oh, how old is he?" asks the mother, breaking the ice with the parent's equivalent of "What's your major?"

"He's going on a year-and-a-half . . . uh, let's see. He just turned sixteen months, I guess." I correct my reply into that new-parent jargon I've been learning from my wife, which defines children's ages in increments of months, weeks, and even days, depending on the need. Parents seem to use this terminology for purposes of comparison, tending to be more vague if their child hasn't reached the same plateau as its peer of the moment. "How old is your boy?"

"Oh, he's a little over eighteen months," she says. "Is yours talking yet?"

I quickly calculate her kid's age into about a year-and-a-half in people years. It makes me feel somewhat relieved to be welcomed into this relatively exclusive club of mothers and children, but at the same time, realizing that this woman is trying to lowball her son's age, I have an uneasy feeling where this conversation is going.

"Yeah, Seth is starting to say a lot of words," I reply, cautiously. "My wife and I really get a kick out of it."

"Really? Well, my Dustin has been talking for months," she says. "We were surprised how fast he picks things up. He talks all the time."

I glance at Dustin, who is strangely silent. One of the neighborhood cats must have his tongue. He does take a keen interest in Seth, however, who is obliviously and deliriously enjoying his ride on the swing.

"It's been quite nice," she continues. "From very early on, we've always been able to understand what Dustin wanted. His older brother was the same way."

"That's nice," I say to her, but I really want to tell her that Seth was working with isosceles triangles in the womb – we knew because we could see him trace them on his mother's belly. Instead, I change the subject, fishing for some information for future reference. "Do you come here often?"

"Oh, yes – Dustin loves it here," she says, just as Dustin

the Articulate prepares to utter his first sound. His keen eye on Seth had become increasingly jaundiced as time went on and suddenly, in response to Seth's laughter, Dustin makes a noise that is half whine and half whimper.

"It's kind of interesting," his mother immediately interjects. "Every time Dustin comes here, he wants to swing on all the swings. I'm not sure exactly why, but we can't go until he has swung on them all."

"Hmmm," is all I can respond, thinking it could be interesting only to a mother and perhaps to the psychoanalyst who tries to unravel Dustin's compulsive behavior someday.

Seth and I say goodbye to the Great Communicator and his mother, and leave the play area altogether, out of fear of what other territory Dustin might have to mark. We wander over to the nearby high school, where some teenagers are practicing on the football field and tennis courts.

As I watch the football players butting heads, knocking each other back and forth to acquire a piece of green real estate, I realize that I don't miss the futile competition of the office place. Every week, we would burn ourselves out putting out a new issue of our newspaper, and nothing earth-shattering ever came from it. Only a handful of letters would trickle in, reminding us that we moved a few readers in our audience. Not enough, I think, to justify having to reacquaint myself with my family at the end of each week.

I glance over at the tennis courts and see a group of high-school girls practicing, and I realize that adult company might come at a premium out here in the suburbs. Suddenly, I miss the busy world of downtown Minneapolis, alive with my working contemporaries. Seeing and being seen is going to be a whole new ballgame in the suburbs.

"Isn't he cute?"

Instinctively, I straighten my posture and look to see which of the tennis players had noticed me. Instead, I see three of the girls giggling and cooing at Seth as he tries to grab a fluorescent green tennis ball through the chain-link fence.

At that moment, I know that I am no longer the focal point of my own daily drama. I am in Seth's world now – he is the star, and I am basically hired help. Here, the competitions are his to win and the spoils his to earn. In the wider world, nothing has really changed – but for me, from here on everything is going to be different.

Chapter 2
Making Mommy Happy

A change of careers is always exciting – the adrenaline rush of new challenges, the interesting confusion of a different routine, the anxious anticipation of the unfamiliar. In my new role, I've found all this and more. When you awaken to a toddler's voice rather than an alarm clock, each day is a step into the unknown.

I've been jazzed about the change. Unfortunately, Lora's role remains unchanged. As we settle into this new stage of our life, for me, everything is exciting and new, and for Lora, it is simply the same. With me going through the changes, however, why is Lora having a hard time adjusting?

After only a few weeks, Lora and I have started to understand what this change will really mean to us. While I've been enjoying the summer with Seth, Lora is struggling to accept the change emotionally. We both know that Lora will have her turn to be the stay-at-home parent (once I get a decent job), but that seems like a far-away goal right now.

So while Lora rides her rollercoaster of emotion, she needs certain things from me. She needs information on her son hourly, she needs to hear that I'm looking for work, and she needs reassurance that she's still the mom. But mostly, she needs to be home with her kid, and since she can't, I need to act like I wish it was her rather than me.

Now, I had anticipated a lot of changes in becoming a househusband, but this is one role I hadn't anticipated: psychological kickball for my stay-at-work wife.

It requires a lot of finesse. I use every bit of my reporting skills to keep her informed of the day's events. But I also need the savvy of a spin doctor to know just how to present those facts. And most importantly, I have to walk the fine line of complaint. If I don't complain, the job will seem too much like the cherry assignment that it can be, but if I complain too much, I look like a wimp.

A typical conversation goes something like this:

"Send out any resumes today?" Lora asks me at supper.

"Uh, no," I reply. "It was so nice out – Seth and I played outside most of the day."

"He does take a nap, you know," she says, stabbing her hotdog with a fork.

"Well, that's when I did the dishes," I say. "It's so tough to get anything done when he's underfoot."

"I'm not going to do this forever, you know," she says. "I want to be home with Seth, too."

"But you always wanted a career," I say, dredging up that old feminist manifesto when it's to my advantage.

"Not after I had a baby," she replies, exercising her womanly prerogative to choose.

"It's not all fun and games here, believe me," I say, as I get up to haul some dirty dishes to the sink.

After a pause, she asks, "Oh, by the way, what was the Final Jeopardy question today?"

"Oh yeah, the category was presidents and the question was real tough," I say, blindsided. "Only the three-day champ and me got it."

"Right, Joe," she says.

Okay, so sometimes it's hard to hide how much I'm enjoying this. But I have had to make some adjustments. Take the kitchen, for instance. Since I'm using it now, shouldn't it be my territory? When we first moved into this house, Lora set the kitchen up the way she wanted it. At the time, I said, "Go right ahead." But I can't find anything in that kitchen. I don't know where anything goes.

For example, Lora separated all the plastic bowls from their lids – all the bowls in a cupboard and all the lids in a drawer. For me, this is a problem: all the covers look the same. Every time I go to find a lid, I have to search for an hour, dirtying every one that touches the food when I try to make it fit. By the time I find one that I can force to fit the bowl, the food is ready to spoil.

> Lora went from being a working-mom to family breadwinner without moving a muscle.

Unfortunately, Lora's adjustment problems are more serious than disorganization among the Tupperware. We knew we would both suffer an identity crisis in our new lives, but hers came first – probably because lack of change allowed her to focus on it. For her, it's like she was standing in the foreground of a photograph and the background changed behind her. She went from being a working-mom to a family breadwinner without moving a muscle.

So now, she acts as though her control as a mom has been supplanted, and she's having a tough time letting it go.

When she comes home from work, she spends the first hour getting reacquainted with Seth – convinced that absence has erased her existence from his memory. We eat supper, I do the dishes, and they play a bit together. Soon, Seth begins playing on his own, and I take an after-dishes break. This is Lora's time to come into the kitchen and apply her own brand of quality control.

"Are these dishes in the dishwasher clean or dirty?" she asks, figuratively tying on an apron. Without waiting for an answer, she checks on it herself and then begins straightening up the counter. "Did you do Seth's laundry today? He's running out of shirts."

As she begins to re-scour the kitchen sink, she starts to reassign the duties I didn't have time for, didn't do well enough, or didn't know needed to be done – just to exert a little power.

"Joe, can you make sure you vacuum the dining room tomorrow? It's starting to look pretty bad. And do the living room, too. And don't you ever clean out the microwave when you do the kitchen?"

The jobs she doesn't want, she guiltlessly subs out. "Can you take out the garbage? I need to spend some time with Seth."

At night, it's even worse. When Seth wakes up, you'd think it would be my job to check on him, since Lora has to go to work in the morning. But not even Olympian Carl Lewis could beat her into the bedroom, should Seth cry out "Mama" at three a.m.

After several bleary-eyed nights standing at Seth's bedroom door watching motherly guilt at work, I got smart. I've perfected a facade of somnambulant struggle, which includes an audible groan, putting one foot on the floor and rolling over in bed while she races out the door. Who am I to keep a mother from her child?

That's what it's like on a good day at our house. The bad days usually come after about four weeknights of interrupted sleep for Seth and his mom, particularly when Lora has a lunch meeting the next day and can't come home for lunch as she usually does, for her noon-time Seth fix. We start our discussion by running the gamut of reasons why this Mister Mom thing isn't working out, why it's not good for Seth, and how much closer he is to leaving home without Lora being his real mom. This discussion usually includes the following statements:

A toddler needs his mother.
A father's a better role model when he's working.
We're going to screw up his gender identity.
He's not going to know me.
He'll always go to you when he's hurt.
He's always going to like you better.
I'm going to miss him growing up.

I refrain from saying that fathers have faced some of these dilemmas for years. My newly enlightened perspective would not be appreciated at that moment.

Instead, I do everything I can to make her feel she's just as involved as I am. Relying on my excellent memory (a reporter's best ally when he's unable to read his own notes), I give her twice daily updates the moment she walks in the door at noon and six p.m. I considered giving her the sports and weather also, until it occurred to me that her office doesn't have windows and she probably doesn't need to be reminded of how gorgeous the summer has been.

My Seth reports usually go over fairly well. Unfortunately, the kid has started racking up the milestones. His vocabulary seems to be increasing daily, and so is Lora's displeasure in me getting all the "firsts" firsthand. I sometimes edit out the minor achievements, to soften the blow.

So when Lora is marveling at Seth's newest animal sound, which I've already heard all morning, I'll stop myself in mid-sentence.

"Oh, he did that . . . just great, honey."

Modern technology is a great help in keeping Lora happy with my Seth reports (and keeping me happily unemployed as a househusband). Every few days, I film Seth with the video camera Lora's father loaned us and play the tapes back during lunchtime. I started by filming Seth playing the toddler's version of baseball in the backyard, but he lost interest when Daddy, tethered by the electrical cord of the camera, didn't want to chase the balls he hit.

No matter, the "dinner and a show" program keeps Lora happy for a minute or two – even though she seems to see through the agenda behind them.

"These tapes are nice, but my memories will be of watching the TV rather than the real events." And then she adds, "Boy, you guys sure must have had fun today."

I quickly improvise – not wanting to jeopardize my summer gig.

"Oh, it wasn't that great," I say, trying to downplay a good time. "He whined a lot. Every time there's an edit, I had to turn off the camera because of a problem. You don't want me to film temper tantrums, do you?"

That's when I crank up the public relations machine. When Lora calls, I put Seth on the phone. When Seth asks for Mommy, I report it as the mantra of the morning. When we hear Mommy's car pull up, I work Seth into such a frenzy of excitement that Lora must think she's won the lottery. And I try to get all the "where Mama's" on camera.

But even these efforts can backfire, depending on the mood of the mother. You see, "where Mama" has two different meanings. When all is right with the world and Mommy has gotten all of her sleep, it means "I love you, Mommy, and I wish you were here." But when work is boring and unfulfilling, it means "Why have you abandoned me, Mommy?"

And it really doesn't matter what kind of spin I try to put on things – Seth holds the power in the situation. While he can't find me a job or bring Lora home, his actions can turn a good lunchtime bad in a hurry. Today, as Lora was heading back to work after lunch, he demonstrated just how powerful he is.

"Mama go," Seth said, running a toy car back and forth across an end table. "Dada home."

Fearing the worst, I looked at the emotions racing across Lora's face and said nothing. So Seth spoke instead.

"Dada go. Mama go," he said, still not bringing a smile to his mother's face.

Then he raced his car one more time across the table, turned to us, grinned, and said triumphantly, "Seth go!" Even Lora had to laugh at this.

In a moment, Seth had turned what was initially interpreted as rejection into something else completely. What it was, we weren't sure, but everything was okay again.

And what an idea – Seth could go to work, and Lora and I could both stay home. Then, everyone would be happy.

Chapter 3
Daddy-Mom

Baby memory books lie. Under "Baby's first words," most parents write things like "Mama," "Dada," "puppy," "ball," or "antidisestablishmentarianism." But let's face it, the first word that a child communicates is "Food!" We just can't understand it.

Whether a baby screams, whines, or babbles a parent's name, it usually means food. In fact, screaming for food is the first thing babies do. And who can blame them? After nine months eating in, the baby is ready to dine out and is usually pretty impatient for its waitress.

From day one, kids want to eat – and they want to eat every succeeding day. So why won't Seth eat for me?

As Seth's daytime-care provider, one of my primary duties is feeding him, but it's the most constant struggle we have. Perhaps I'm not understanding him, but I swear it takes an alchemist to figure out what to feed a toddler to make sure he gets nutritious, satisfying sustenance. Eating shouldn't be such a problem for the little guy – it's a major focus of his day, the thing he spends the most time thinking about, talking about, and doing.

Just a few months ago, all Seth got was bottles of formula, bland rice cereal, and multi-colored jars of mush. Maybe his preferences then should have been our first clue he was going to be a fussy eater. As a baby, Seth turned up his little nose at the apple juice that every other nine-month-old sucks down like they're inhaling pure oxygen. And not a single spoonful of strained pears was ever allowed past his pearly white baby teeth – rather than swallowing fruit, he let it dribble down his chin.

But now that he's got a good set of teeth and a rough ability to get food from his plate to his mouth by himself, almost everything we eat should be fair game for him. After all, Dad knows how to cook with sugar and salt – after his previous diet, what more could Seth want?

When we first opened the floodgates to big people food, Seth was pretty experimental (except for fruit). One night, Lora was gone and I served the blood sausage that Seth's Grandpa Tony provided. Now, Lora doesn't let me eat blood sausage in the same house as her, but Seth had me scraping the sausage casing for more.

Another night, I made tacos and broccoli. I mixed it around on Seth's plate, and we named the colorful result "braccos" – he ate every bite. In fact, he loves broccoli, a rarity in a kid. We call them "little trees," and he shoves them into his mouth foliage-first.

But somewhere along the line, Seth fell off course – all three courses. He's no longer interested in the carefully balanced meals I struggle to feed him, and I've became more and more panicked about his nutrition.

With every meal, I put carefully cut-up bananas, grapes, or apples in a bowl next to his plate – they end up as shriveled bits in the garbage by the end of the day. He won't drink milk from a cup, only a bottle – although he does love water and will carry a sippy-cup full of it around with him all day.

As far as bread and cereals go, Seth must think that this food group consists of Cheerios and french fries. Thank heavens that he still loves broccoli, even though it's the only vegetable he'll eat.

Seth has three favorite lunchtime meals that he'd live on, if I'd let him: Kraft macaroni and cheese, Campbell's bean and bacon soup, and a plateful of meat and cheese. The other day, I looked at the lunch I had prepared for him – a piece of salami, a slice of cheese, and a glass of water. I felt like the warden of a prison camp.

I try to make other types of food interesting to him. "Here comes the airplane" accompanying a spoonful of green beans still won't get them into the hangar. One day, in desperation, I even tried feeding him apple slices with his favorite plastic pliers. He laughed uproariously, but wouldn't eat them. For me, every little portion of grape that makes it past his teeth is like a tiny vitamin that could somehow save his fruit-starved body.

This finickiness seemed to intensify about the time Seth became able to talk. Seth has always been able to show his displeasure for certain foods – now, he can articulate it, as well. Before, he just tipped his plate onto the floor; now, he whines "yucchy" and then tips it onto the floor. Unfortunately, he isn't as clear at saying what he *does* want.

I worry, though, that his fussiness may be more than just a simple communication problem between Seth and me. Maybe my new role has affected his eating paradigm in some strange, cosmic way. (Of course, this excuse occurs to me no matter what little problem crops up.)

Since day one, Lora has been Seth's main-person, his major source of food, a soothing voice, and comforting caresses. Lora had the grub, and when "Mama" became part of his lexicon, it was like the sound of a dinner bell. "Dada" came out of his mouth first, but he's always said "Mama" more often.

Nowadays, the dinner bell rings to the tune of "Dada" – what does that do to a year-and-a-half's worth of Pavlovian training? The traditional hunter/gatherer in our family is now the cooker/feeder at Seth's table. What would Joseph Campbell think of that? I had expected a period of transition as we converted to this new lifestyle, but I never expected this.

You see, Seth is having a little trouble distinguishing between our names lately. "Mama," he said, looking directly at me. "Seth hungry."

I don't mind doing this househusband job, but I won't wear an apron and I don't want to be called Mama.

Yet, that's exactly what my one-year-old son has been doing. Sure, from time to time, Seth mimics Lora and calls me "Doe" for Joe (sometimes it comes out "DoeDoe"), but the use of Dada has fallen way down on his list. I suppose I could tolerate being called Mom if he put Mister in front of it, but a toddler's hunger evokes cries of panic sooner than a multi-syllabic movie title.

Lora was no help at first. She just giggled at my discomfort – her small revenge at me being the one home with Seth. But one day, Seth called her Dada. Then, the fun was over.

The next few mealtimes we spent doing conditioning drills on who's who in our household.

"Who's that?" Lora would begin, pointing to me and using her best game-playing voice.

"Dada," Seth responded promptly.

"And who's that?" I jumped in, pointing to Lora.

"Mama," Seth was enjoying this.

"And who's that?" Lora grabbed the momentum and pointed at the culprit himself.

"Seth," he said in his high, piping lisp, collapsing into a fit of giggles.

Of course, Seth knows who we are when asked point-blank, but under the stress of communicating, all kinds of things slip out. And as his vocabulary grows, he's begun combining our names, especially when he's not looking at us while talking. I get called "Mommydad," or sometimes "Mahdaddy." Lora is "Daddymom" or "Damom." Neither Lora nor I can tell if he's made a mistake or is just messing with our minds.

But it *is* highly efficient. When there's a dire need to be satisfied, Seth can just bellow combinations of the two names in rapid, vociferous succession until he gets some attention. It always works.

It makes me wonder what's going on in his mind. Could Shakespeare be right – you know, "a rose by any other name still smells as sweet"? Hunger apparently means the same thing to Seth whether he calls it Mama or Dada.

On the other hand, maybe he really is confusing traditional gender roles and we're raising a boy who will someday take time out from watching the Super Bowl to do the dishes. Only time will tell.

I guess the important thing is that Seth knows he'll keep getting his food, no matter what name he calls or who brings it to him. It might end up being blood sausage and braccos served on a plastic pliers for a while, though. Because until he gets my name right, I won't be taking him out to any restaurants.

Chapter 4

Braving the New World

The world may not yet be ready for stay-at-home dads – at least, that's how it seems to me. Sure, the newspaper, magazines, and TV periodically run pieces – usually around Father's Day – proclaiming that more and more fathers are giving up careers and staying home with their children. But who besides the lonely househusband really pays attention to them?

To people unaccustomed with the Mister Mom phenomenon, I'm a bit of an anomaly, more easily categorized as a lazy unemployed slob with a saint for a wife. Or so some of the looks I get around town would have me believe.

We live in an older, working-class suburb where most of the residents have already raised their families and, instead of changing diapers, are spending their spare time working a second job to pay for car insurance for their twenty-something kids – who are running around with the kind of freedom I used to have. Most of our neighbors seem more like my parents' contemporaries than mine. When they raised their kids, the women were housewives and the men were . . . well, employed.

Yup, things are pretty traditional in our town. At our local grocery store, middle-aged women push shopping carts and run the checkouts; high-school kids retrieve carts from the parking lot and stock the shelves. Women and teenagers hustle the fast-food, assist you in your purchases at the local mall, and take your money at the bank. Men run the service stations, drive forklifts at the lumber yard, manage the local sports bars, and sell tires at the tire shop. Manly stuff.

So when a person such as myself – a male in his mid-thirties with a small son in tow – buys groceries or picks up drycleaning during the workday, there are more double-takes and sideways glances than a cat would get in a dog pound. The enlightened world of magazine Father's Day cover stories feels like a galaxy away. And, as a hypersensitive househusband, I can only wish Scotty would beam me there.

A Mister Mom never knows exactly what reaction he's going to get. The response I like best is the cooing of women who think Seth is adorable and don't care about my situation. The tellers at my bank, for example, always have a lollipop for Seth and a child-raising story to swap with me. They seem genuinely interested in my stories – probably because they can see I'm clearly a fish out of water.

Other times, I run into working mothers who – maybe because they're away from their child during the day – seem to want to prove that their mothering skills are superior to mine. Seth and I took the car to the gas station, and the girl working behind the counter was a parent much younger than myself. Seth, just calming down from a mini-tantrum, had a pacifier in his mouth.

"How old is your boy?" she asked about Seth, whom I held in one arm.

"About a year-and-a-half," I said.

"Oh, that's the same age as my boy," she said. "You know, he gave up his Nuk a long time ago" (Please note: "a long time ago" is vague parentspeak – it actually could have been last week.)

"Really," I said, but I wanted to lean across the counter, take her by the lapels, and say, "My boy is using his to quit smoking – that's a tough habit to break, you know."

Other mothers just look astonished to see a man interacting

with a child at all. I took Seth to the local indoor recreation center with its bouncing, jumping, swinging, crawling, sliding, and tumbling apparati. The mothers stared curiously at me as I chaperoned Seth through the various play areas. I guess I stuck out as the only adult male in the crowd – but I stuck out even worse as the only overgrown kid whipping down the slide into a pile of plastic balls.

The worst response is the kind I got from the checker at the grocery store, a woman about the same age as my mother. I could see that she was studying Seth and me as we placed our food on the checkout counter, paid for it, and began bagging the groceries. She was clearly trying to figure out what I was doing buying food without a woman's help. Before she gave me the receipt, she decided to give me her thoughts.

"I would never let my husband shop for groceries," she said. "I'm afraid of what he'd bring home."

I politely chuckled and thought about reminding her that, since she worked in a grocery store, she was probably better situated to handle the shopping. But instead I mentally shrugged it off and said, "My wife was that way, too, when we first got married. But then we shopped together enough for her to trust me."

"He was laid off," she said, after a pause, referring to her husband. "Were you?"

Clearly caught off guard, I quickly mumbled a lie: "Yes," I said, not wanting to go into a long explanation of how I had left my job voluntarily but was still kind of working freelance. And anyway, it wasn't completely untrue – I had been laid off in the past.

"I know there's nothing he can do about it, but it drives me nuts to have him around the house all day," she said.

"Yeah," I said, grabbing the receipt. "Thanks."

From then on, I've made it a point to go to checkout counters with young girls who like to giggle at Seth and ignore me – no matter how long the wait in line.

I changed my routine in other ways as well, making trips to service stations and other male-staffed places only during the evening or on weekends. The fewer trips out of my home during the day, the better. The only problem is explaining to Lora why I never get any errands run during the day.

Still, the home is no oasis from the chastising looks of an uncomprehending public. The outside world has a way of intruding on the househusband's little sanctuary.

Simple upkeep of a home occasionally requires some outside help, and Lora and I just happen to be doing some redecorating and fixing up right now. From the electrician and upholstery cleaners to the telephone installer and wallpaper hanger, everyone who comes into our home has made me feel just a slight bit on edge.

The electrician was closed-mouth as he wired a new light in our basement stairway. He seemed unsure what to think of me cooking macaroni and cheese and doing the dishes while he drilled holes in our wall. Since I had rehabbed a house in my distant, pre-fatherhood past, I questioned him about the two-way switch he was installing – just to show I knew the lingo.

I was also quick to point out the stripping and painting I had done in the very spot he was working. Still, he was unimpressed, and I was a bit unnerved.

The upholstery cleaners came into the house three men strong – which, by the way, outnumbered the pieces of furniture that I wanted cleaned. Apparently, the boss was needed to sit with me and talk about the bill, while trying to sell me more of his company's service.

Seth was a bit fussy that day, and after I settled him down, I sheepishly said, "Oh, I love my job."

"You'd probably rather be golfing," the crew boss said, laughing, obviously thinking I was on vacation.

"Actually, I would rather be working," I said and chased after Seth as he ran toward the big bucket of chemicals the cleaners were pouring into their equipment.

It turned out that the crew boss's mom owned the business. Now, if I thought that working for a female-owned business would make him more understanding of my situation, I was wrong. He made the bill out to Mrs. Oberle, as if I wasn't even there. Force of habit, I guess.

This assumption is not unique to upholstery cleaners – every phone solicitor who calls during the weekday asks for Lora. And although it helps to get rid of them sooner when I say she's not home, that doesn't help my ego at all.

> When a man selling aluminum siding called and asked if I was Mrs. Oberle, my fun came to an abrupt halt.

When I complained about this to a housewife friend of mine, she explained that the calls always come for the woman of the house, but the bill always arrives made out to the man – a practice that burns her to no end.

I must really confuse the heck out of phone solicitors because they usually *do* hang up and call back for Lora. But when a man selling aluminum siding asked if *I* was Mrs. Oberle, my fun came to an abrupt halt. I considered three responses at that point:

1) saying, "This is *Mr.* Oberle – who do I sound like, Michael Jackson?"

2) banging the receiver on the nearest blunt object and yelling, "Is this phone not working here? Do we have a bad connection?"

3) politely chuckling and saying, "No, this is *Mr.* Oberle, but I'm the woman of the house, so I'll buy the most expensive of whatever it is you're selling."

I wanted to cry sexism – or reverse sexism – or something, and then ask this guy what exactly he thought my wife knew about aluminum siding. (In fact, she knows as much as I do – which is nothing – but he didn't know that.) Instead, I was short with him, but civil, because I have my own problems with gender roles.

You see, the telephone company sent over a petite phone

installer named Dawn to install our new phone jack (a job that I didn't have the right tools to do). Instead, I moved boxes out of her way, carried her ladder, and held the door open for her. When she was all set to work, I told her that if she needed me, I would be outside mowing the lawn, chopping wood, or breaking something with a sledgehammer.

I was lucky, because Dawn didn't seem to mind my help. She politely explained that some of the floor joists she had to drill through were hard to reach for a woman her size. Another woman might have objected to my assistance and labelled me patronizing, condescending, sexist, or psychologically upsetting – when in fact, it was my male psyche that was reeling and needed support.

The final straw was Mary the Wallpaperer. Mary reminded me of my mother, a middle-aged woman with grown children who now works full-time and loves it. She did a great job with the wallpaper, too, but it was incredibly awkward for me. Here I was, a full-grown, able-bodied man, sitting on my couch watching "Sesame Street" while this mother-substitute hung wallpaper in my bathroom. Of course, I was "helping" by keeping Seth out of her way, but my ego didn't buy that for a minute.

Before Mary arrived, I had prepared the walls by stripping, spackling, and sanding them top to bottom. Now, I felt a strong desire to do them all over again, right in front of her.

Instead, I helped Mary move furniture, asked about her technique, and bragged desperately about all the backbreaking work I had done on the rehabbed house. Mary was more interested in hearing about what kind of sleeper Seth was and if I had started to potty train him.

It had been Lora's idea to have someone else do our wallpapering. When I rehabbed that old house, I had done just about everything but wallpapering, and Lora didn't trust me to learn it on our house. Unfortunately, when Lora hired a wallpaperer, she neglected to tell me that she had hired a woman – and a talkative one at that.

When lunchtime arrived, I felt compelled to invite Mary

to eat with us. I never in my life expected to be sitting across the dining-room table from a handywoman in paint-stained pants discussing meal alternatives for toddlers.

That weekend, when Mary came to finish the job, Lora was there so I made myself scarce. I told them I'd be calling around to find a good shrink specializing in gender roles, identity, and male ego.

This week, however, I found solace. Seth and I had gone to the bank with the allowance check Lora gives me for groceries. As I struggled to strap Seth in his stroller, out the door of the bank came a father about my age with a daughter a little older than Seth. Spotting us, the father waited, holding the door for the stroller.

I looked at him and thanked him; instead of the usual Minnesotan response – "You betcha!" – he gave me an all-knowing nod and a smile.

He could have done no more for me if he had laid his hands upon me and said, "Be healed." I was no longer alone. There actually was another one of me out there, and he already knew we had to stick together. I wondered if we should form a support group – or apply for minority status.

I might be confused about this "who am I now that I'm home" stuff, but I have a compadre, a brother househusband. It's only a matter of time before we stay-at-home dads get the respect we deserve.

Right?

Chapter 5
Books, Balls, and Automobiles

The first day of Seth's life was one of the best days of my life. Beginning with his birth at 10:50 p.m., I spent several exhausted and ecstatic midnight hours in the hospital nursery, simply staring and marveling at this brand-new bundle of greatness.

They say when you die, your whole life flashes before your eyes; well, when your child is born, his or her potential life races through your mind. Seth was just minutes old, but he grabbed my finger with such a strong grip that I dreamed of him catching the winning pass in the Super Bowl, sometime in the next millennium.

I ran to the recovery room to see Lora, who was trying to rally from Caesarean section surgery and wanted little to do with me or my rapid-fire reports on every movement Seth made. Punctuating each half-sentence with a dry heave caused by the anesthetic, Lora told me – as kindly as possible – to "get the heck away from me."

So I returned to Seth until the wee hours of the morning, when we both needed to get some sleep. I left, but slept little and returned early the next day.

On Seth's first full day here on earth, I held him in my arms, and we watched the state high-school hockey tournament on TV. I took it as a good omen that Seth never asked me to change the channel. My daydreams about his future sports career continued until Lora's nurse came into the hospital room and brought a quick halt to my thoughts.

"I like hockey, too," she said, as she gave Lora her lunch. "But I'll tell you, hockey is so competitive in Minneapolis that you have to start the kids very early."

I quietly thought it might be okay to let him master walking before I strapped him into a pair of CCM Tacks, but she had a point. Minnesota *is* hockey mad.

"Yeah," I agreed, "you've got to start them skating young."

"Oh, but the worst thing is the parents," she said. "They're the worst sports parents of all. There's so much politics and in-fighting and bad feelings that my husband and I stopped being involved."

The nurse had struck a nerve. I'm the son of a sports enthusiast who provided every opportunity for his children to play sports, and I knew that my own desires for Seth's future would have to be monitored, if not checked.

Of course, my dad never pushed me. He didn't have to – keeping up with my older brother, Bob, was incentive enough. Instead, Dad encouraged all five of his children by investing his time and interest in our sports careers. He coached our teams and bought us equipment, even installing a mini-sports complex in our backyard, complete with hockey rink, whiffle-ball field, pitching backstop, football field, golf/marbles hole, and basketball court.

I told myself that I would do no more (or was it less?) and resumed watching the hockey tournament.

Now, a year-and-a-half later, it's good for me to recall that conversation with the nurse. As househusband and primary caregiver for Seth, my power and influence in my son's life is extensive. With Lora away at work all day and me home with Seth, I have ample opportunity to mold him any way I please.

Since I secretly fear that I'm a confusing role model for the young lad, it seems even more important to expose him to a little sports. So I bought him a few sporting items to whet his appetite – what are ten or twenty little balls going to hurt? Besides, my rule of thumb for shopping has always been to shop what you know, and I don't know anything about buying dolls for boys.

In fact, the first gift I ever bought for Seth was a small, soft Vikings football. My politically correct friends told me I was perpetuating a gender stereotype, but I defended the move by saying I would have bought the football even if Seth had been a girl. The sad thing is, that's the truth – I had bought it before he was born.

Seth was four months old and barely able to prop himself up on his elbows when he first took an interest in that football. I was playing with him on the family-room floor, and the ball inadvertently rolled into his cupped hands. I was convinced we had given birth to the next Jerry Rice.

Later, when he first rolled it back to me – the first game of catch between father and son – I was sure of the course his life would take: sports.

What I hadn't noticed in the meantime was that Seth's aunts, uncles, grandparents, and mother had been buying him a lot of other toys. And there seemed to be two themes behind them all: books and cars.

Books aren't a problem – as a kid, I read lots of sports books, with memorable names like *Touchdown for Tommy*. In Seth's later years, there will be the daily newspaper sports page, *Sports Illustrated*, and sports hero biographies. So, books are not a threat to my plans – only to the time needed to carry them out.

A fellow parent once told me, "You can never read to them enough." At the time, I thought he was saying that a parent can never do too much to educate his children, and I readily agreed. Since I've become a stay-at-home parent, though, I've discovered what he really meant – you can never read enough to satisfy them.

As a writer, I don't want to back down from a request for a bit of reading time with Seth. Dear God, please stun me with a lightning bolt if I ever utter the words, "You've got that one on tape, Seth. Why don't you go watch it on TV?"

Still, seven back-to-back readings of *Hop on Pop* can get a little tiresome. It's hard to bring the same excitement and surprise to each recitation of Mr. Brown's triumphant return to town with Mr. Black.

The seventh reading is usually the magic number when the book becomes a rectangular Frisbee sailed across the room. (Not unlike Mr. Brown being catapulted out of town.) Just the distraction needed to get Seth throwing other things – like balls, for instance.

I didn't realize the effect that all the reading was having on me until I attended my fantasy football draft last week. A player named Ned was announced for selection, and it was unclear whether Ned was his first or last name, so it was repeated back and forth several times.

I didn't want Ned, so I perused my own list of players while the argument continued. Absent-mindedly, I muttered – more audibly than I'd suspected – "Ned Bed. Red, Ned, Ted and Ed in bed."

Across the room, another parent heard me and said, "Joe, you have to get out of the house more often."

But, books really are not a problem. I don't mind taking time out from playing ball to read them. If either Seth or I get tired of one, we can always buy another one – a vicious financial cycle that Lora and I never hesitate to perpetuate.

The problem is cars. Cars, trucks, and vehicles of any sort or configuration. Rolling balls have never held Seth's fascination as much as rolling wheels.

Seth drives his cars everywhere. He pushes them across the floor, along the contours of our overstuffed couch (to simulate mountain terrain), on the bathroom vanity (near the lake, that is), and all around the dining-room table. He lines them up as if they were in the longest single-lane parking lot in the world, and then he runs one by the group, watching each rotation of the wheels as it goes.

It's trancelike, the way he watches his cars. Most of the time he doesn't even make motor sounds. Instead, he silently moves them into straight lines, in mystical communion with the universe of wheels.

Whenever I join Seth in playing cars, I'm always unsure which car to push. Playing ball, I know our roles: throwing and catching and throwing again. But car games are different every time you play them, and Seth's seem to have predetermined rules that I haven't figured out yet.

Cars are pretty butch, so his fascination with them soothes my anxiety over being a masculine role model. My problem is that they usurp our community in sports. Our games of catch peter off in disinterest, and Seth gravitates toward his cars. The battle for my son's attention has ensued, and ESPN and I are already behind.

My vision of his future knocking in the winning run of the World Series began to evaporate into the visible heat rising from the pavement of the Indianapolis 500 race track.

My vision of his future knocking in the winning run of the World Series has begun to evaporate into the visible heat rising from the blistering pavement of the Indianapolis 500 track. There he is, dressed head-to-toe in a red, advertisement-laden jumpsuit, cranking off the wheels of Mario Andretti's grandson's car. And there I am in the stands, with my radio headphones and a miniature TV, listening to baseball and watching a golf tournament.

It's not that car racing or auto repair are bad occupations – it's just that they're more butch than I am. I've changed my oil, filled my windshield-washer well, assisted in a friend's brake job, changed countless flat tires, and even jerry-rigged a rusted muffler, but all at financial gunpoint – only the threat of bankruptcy has moved me to do my own auto repair.

Since I've never had that much of an interest in cars, future family reunion discussions will be tough, having to talk about the latest alternator rebuild job Seth has done. My only consolation is the thought of free car maintenance.

Since Seth's love of cars is so obvious, he's built up quite the collection. For Christmas and his birthday, his relatives have given him big plastic Tonka construction vehicles and sporty little Hot Wheels race cars, fire trucks that supply their own sound effects, and assorted sets of forty-plus cars and trucks. It's so bad that I had to dig deep into his toy box to find the plastic ball and bat that *I* bought him.

It's not hard to imagine where Seth will be spending his time after school when he reaches high-school age – in the garage with his car. My dad wouldn't let me buy a car when I got my driver's license because he feared I'd spend all my time working on it instead of going to football practice. I figure somehow I'm going to have to keep Seth from building a car of his own from scratch before he's old enough to drive it.

What it comes down to is that my influence means little to nothing. I might be home with him all day, with enough authority to direct his activities to my liking, but that's not enough to mold his interests. Sports are okay for a diversion, but cars are his life, and that feeling comes from inside him, not from me.

What's more, his passion seems to be changing my own interest in cars. I find myself wondering why I didn't build model cars as a kid or meandering out to the garage to see if our minivan needs a wash. Not only am I not creating a miniature me, but Seth is drawing me into his little world of Hot Wheels, Matchbox cars, and snippy little Thomas the Tank Engines.

I'm happy to report that my mini-revelation has improved things around the house. Seth and I have discovered a new game that we both enjoy playing. It's a little game of compromise that I like to call "Carball." After we line up all his cars in a row, we take all the balls in the house and throw them at the cars. We both love it. I think he's going to be a star.

If memory serves, more than one great quarterback got his start throwing footballs through a tire.

Part II
Fall

Househusband Questions

Why, if your kid doesn't want to get into the bathtub, does he then not want to get out?

Why, every morning, do you have to wrestle the pajamas off the child that you had to tie them onto the night before?

When a child gets his diaper changed, his legs are bent back over his head, his pants are pulled down, and someone is rubbing cold, stinging, wet stuff across his red, sore skin. So why would a kid want to wear diapers any longer than he has to?

How come a child sleeps so lightly at home in his comfortable bed that you have to tip-toe past his door in fear that a slight creak of a floorboard will bring on a half-hour screaming tantrum, when he'll fall fast asleep in your arms at church, neck uncomfortably craned over your shoulder, while a priest shouts a sinner-be-saved sermon from the pulpit and a thirty-member choir belts out the latest in rock'n'roll hymns?

How come a child treats warm bathwater being poured over his head to wash his hair like a hydrochloric acid rinse, when he'll gladly douse himself with ice-cold water from the backyard pool?

Chapter 6

What Was Yours Is Mine and What Was Mine, Still Is

When Lora and I were first married, we never assumed that our domestic duties would fall into typical gender-defined roles, but they did. Even though we both cooked, she handled the kitchen and cleaning, and I did all the mowing, shoveling, raking, repairing, and unclogging sewer drains. At the time, I would have felt no more at ease asking her to take out the garbage than asking her to jackhammer up some unwanted patio concrete. We were a '90s couple – whatever that means – but we were practical and knew each other's strengths.

So it shouldn't have been a surprise – although it was – that when we switched roles my list of household duties got longer and hers got suspiciously shorter. Call me naive, but I had expected the change to be more of an *ex*change. Much to my chagrin, however, I've noticed that not all is as I had thought it would be. In addition to my new chores of cooking, cleaning, and laundry, I've retained the outdoor jobs.

Don't get me wrong – I fully intended to hold on to some traditional male functions, like belching the loudest, watching sports on TV, and supplying the Y chromosome needed in child conception. But I was under the impression that the rest of the role reversal should be relatively consistent.

Since it's now my job to dust, it only makes sense that

Lora should carry in wood for the fireplace. Of course, I never actually *do* dust, but then, we only have fires during the winter.

Similarly, now that cleaning the toilet, bathtub, and bathroom sink falls under my job description, shouldn't plumbing problems be relegated to the breadwinner? After all, she's making the money that allows her to call a plumber.

But this is not the case in our household. The chores have fallen into their own strange new pattern that neither of us can quite put a finger on. Sometimes gender applies, sometimes it doesn't – especially when it's something Lora doesn't want to do, like scrubbing the toilet. Sometimes the working mother likes to control the vision behind the project – she won't let me reorganize her kitchen, for example – but the househusband still does the actual work. And other times the chore is technically mine, but nobody really does it (like dusting).

Everything having to do with food has become my job. I cook the meals, clean the dishes, vacuum up the crumbs, and do the grocery shopping. Lora cooks us Sunday morning breakfasts, once the staple of traditional 1950s-style fathers.

Other duties that traditionally belong to the man of the house are still mine, however. I not only sweep and vacuum, but I care for the outdoor flooring, too: raking, mowing, and probably shoveling, too.

Since I'm not sure exactly which are my duties and which aren't, I mostly just do as much as possible, so I can cover my tail. The guilt of the out-of-work husband and father knows no bounds, even when it comes to scrubbing soap scum off the bathroom tile. (Name one bachelor who ever did that.)

I'm never confused about who handles the money in our house, though. Lora has made that perfectly clear – whoever makes it, manages it. She brings the money into the home, so she generally decides where it goes from there. It's gotten to the point where she reads the financial magazines and leaves *Good Housekeeping* for me – and I, unwittingly, read it.

When it comes to be that time of the month – bill-paying time – I feel like cowering in a corner like an incontinent dog.

Each month, I painfully wait in silence as the monthly budget is figured out. The silence that follows her reading of the bottom line is loud and clear: "I know this is what we decided to do, but you promised to do some freelance work and you're not bringing in enough money."

After the discussion that follows, I usually scurry to the kitchen, where I can always find more cleaning to do. Unfortunately, then I also discover the empty refrigerator. That forces me to engage in my most humiliating ritual of being a househusband: asking for my periodic allowance to go grocery shopping.

Lora always responds to my request as if she somehow believes I'd find a way to buy groceries without money. I feel like I should approach her on bended knee, propping a gaunt and droopy-eyed Seth nearby to illustrate my case. Threatening to get the money by walking the streets falls on deaf ears, and she grudgingly hands it over like she's lost some kind of bet.

How many times have I shrugged off my mom's complaint about not getting paid for housework? Never again.

But I don't want it to seem like I'm too hard on Lora. After getting up at night to check on Seth, she manages to stumble out of bed every morning and make it to work, where she puts in long hours, worrying that she's becoming a footnote in her son's life. When the money is that hard-earned, it's reasonable for her to want it to stretch farther.

And in the evening, what with running the finances, checking up on me, and trying to find time for Seth, her plate is full. So if she forgets to take it to the sink after dinner, waltzing instead into the family room like it's my job to clear the table – who am I to complain? If she's too tired to cook even on weekends, why should that matter? If time with her son is more important than time behind a lawn mower, can I really say "Get to work!"?

And if the truth be known, I don't mind hanging on to the traditional male jobs. No self-respecting man can stay chained to the kitchen forever. They'd take his "Guy" card away if he was ever caught uttering the phrase: "Uh, no, I can't go mow the lawn right now. I've got a basket full of socks to darn."

A guy needs to get out in the garage every once in a while, turn on the radio to Sports Talk, and rut around – even if it's only to take a tool inventory and have a couple of beers. It helps the weary househusband feel like a man and reminds his wife of that fact also. Let's face it, most woman would rather be caressed by callused hands than rough, red dishpan ones.

It's just that Lora fell into the inequity of our new roles so easily. By her own admission, she started out wanting to do everything: work, homemake, and mother. Then she discovered that I wasn't totally incompetent, and she started to feel useless. Now, she plainly enjoys being served dinner, having her dishes cleared and washed, her laundry done and her bed made – it gives her more time to pay the bills, after all.

Lora admits feeling guilty about it, but the routine is just too pleasant for her to change it. And she knows that I'm in no position to demand anything of her. As I said before, guilt is a powerful motivator when it comes to household chores.

They say a man's home is his castle, but a househusband will take a ranch house when he's got to clean the damn thing. We've settled into our new roles and pretty much made them ours – I just hope to God that Lora hasn't settled in permanently.

Chapter 7
Cheerios Everywhere

General Mills must be happy. Cheerios, its star product, seems to be the meal of choice among the pre-sentence set. Nearly every infant with a few choppers spends mornings cramming Cheerios in its mouth; most toddlers on three wheels are driving around with oat breath. Everywhere they go, little trails of free advertising are left behind – and Seth eats enough to be pictured on the Cheerios box.

But why Cheerios? With grocery-store aisles stacked to the roof with sugar-filled, marshmallowy, rainbow-colored breakfast cereals, why does every kid ever born devour Cheerios like a piranha in a wading pool? It was a question that puzzled me from the moment Seth started to eat solid foods – and even more so when I came home to be the one feeding him. Was Cheerios doctor-recommended? Or was it some trade secret passed between mothers? How did Lora know to start buying Cheerios? Was she just taken in by good advertising? My reporter's instincts were piqued, and I was determined to figure it out.

I had not been a househusband for long before I began to learn more about Cheerios. The little round O's were everywhere – on the bathroom floor, in the toy box, between seat cushions, and down every hallway. Scattered Cheerios dotted the terrain like insect life preservers. The vacuum cleaner was soon filled with them, and I began to wonder which got more, Seth or the Hoover.

But I also began to suspect that many of these spilled Cheerios were left behind on purpose. On one long car trip, I happened to glance into the back seat to discover Seth happily munching away – and I knew I hadn't given him anything to eat. That was when I learned that Seth's carseat held a veritable cache of Cheerios. Since then, I've never cleaned out any stray Cheerios sitting in the corners of his seat: I leave them behind for emergencies.

Was it hereditary, I wondered, was Seth a third-generation Cheerios muncher? I knew that Cheerios was my only morning menu choice until I was about six or seven years old, when I had both the flu and Cheerios for breakfast. (I couldn't go near them for years after that.) Had Cheerios been around for my mom to grow up on, and had she forced her tastes onto me? My dad, who grew up on a farm, always had eggs and bacon for breakfast, so it couldn't be ancestral on his side.

Of course, masterful marketing is part of the story – General Mills' advertising has certainly helped keep the nation's children munching doughnut-shaped oats. For instance, while many mothers keep little plastic bags full of Cheerios in their purses or diaper bags, we have a round plastic container specifically designed for transporting a late breakfast. Marketed by General Mills, it is shaped like a Cheerio and is bright yellow like the cereal box, guaranteed to make Seth salivate on sight no matter what the time of day.

In fact, I keep expecting General Mills to come out with the slogan that Cheerios aren't just for breakfast anymore. Seth eats them any time of the day (and would eat them in bed, if we'd let him). Sometimes I think that it's like an addiction – you dare not run out of Cheerios or else you'd better prepare for the inevitable tantrum. Then again, a tantrum is just what the sight of Cheerios can magically stop.

Take, for instance, church – where children's tantrums live. In our church, the fire and brimstone of the pulpit is frequently bested by the anger and wrath of the cryroom. But not with Cheerios along. When Seth isn't rolling the little oat wheels along the back of the pew in front of us, he sits back, restfully taking in the sermon and a few O's. But even that doesn't guarantee peace.

On one trip to Sunday Mass, Seth decided to eat his breakfast in the cryroom. As he lay back in Lora's arms, relishing his Cheerios like a wino with a bottle, the boy in his mother's arms in front of Seth eyed him carefully. In slovenly handfuls, Seth stuffed his mouth, moaning with oral satisfaction. Each of Seth's groans caused the boy's eyes to widen until tears began appearing around the edges.

If you are without Cheerios, someone else will have some. Next time, you will help out. It was like cereal socialism.

The boy whimpered, catching his mother's attention, and she turned to discern the problem. I asked her if he would like some Cheerios. "Oh, yes, thank you," she replied. "He has a container like that at home."

With a soggy little hand, Seth offered one Cheerio to the boy, like he was handing out communion, and I wondered if the whole child congregation would soon be queuing up. At that moment, a whole new facet of the Cheerios phenomenon opened up before me. As a safeguard from tantrums, Cheerios was a common ground for all mothers. And if you are without Cheerios this time, someone else will have some. Next time, you will help out – it was like cereal socialism.

Okay, fair enough, but, still, why Cheerios in particular? Why not another cereal? I answered that question a couple of weeks later. The Cheerios in our house were gone, and Seth and I were late for Mass. I hurriedly filled the plastic container with Rice Krispies and raced off to the church. Thankfully, Seth liked the Rice Krispies, and he noisily shoved them in his mouth while sitting on my lap.

But strangely enough, no one eyed us in envy. In fact, several nearby families recoiled slightly in their seats and slid down the pew at the first sight of the Rice Krispies. Smaller and weaker than the mighty Cheerio, the little krispies flew like feathers from a pillow as Seth ate – there were cereal particles and dust everywhere. I struggled to retrieve them as Seth stuffed more in his mouth, catching what I could of the cereal squirting between his fingers.

When I stood up, Rice Krispies fell off me like drops of sweat, and I spent the standing portion of Mass on my knees cleaning the carpet. On our way back from communion, the two of us left small cereal droppings behind in the aisle. We made an early exit – but not before I vowed to never again bring Rice Krispies to church.

I have finally reached my conclusion about Cheerios, and it's really brilliantly simple: They hold together better than other cereals (you should see the Wheaties crumbs in my car), and kids like them. There's nothing more mysterious than that. When I finally asked Lora about it, she told me as much. I should have asked sooner.

Of course, just when I figured it all out, I discovered a new problem: Seth likes milk on his Cheerios.

Chapter 8
Just Practicing Entropy

Before I got married, I lived in a house with several other bachelors. One housemate, John, always did his share to clean up the rest of the house, but that must have tired him out because his own room was constantly in shambles. When called on it, John would justify the mess in one sentence: "I'm just practicing entropy."

The theory of entropy, according to John's college physics class, states that all things tend toward chaos. Since John's room was always headed in the direction of disorder, he decided that the cost of the energy spent to put it back in order was a waste. After all, no one can ever win the battle against entropy.

As the father of a toddler, I finally agree with John. Seth is the embodiment of the theory of entropy. He is a constant practitioner.

Seth seems to have John's attitude about an orderly room – he just isn't concerned about it. When I ask him to pick up his toys, he looks at me as if to say, "Why pick them up, Dad? I'm just going to take them out and put them on the floor again."

As entropic a thought as ever I've heard.

And how can I blame him? Cleaning up his toys is a monumental chore. One major difference between having a child in daycare and staying home with your child is the amount of time the child has to distribute toys throughout the house.

Seth leaves his toys everywhere. When he brings the Duplos out to play, he dumps them and then walks through them, spreading them around the room like a dog stalking around his bed before he lies in it. Seth may not want to play with these particular toys, of course – they are for atmosphere. You see, the room just feels more comfortable to him when it's messed up. If there is a toy within reaching distance anywhere in the room, it's ready for play.

I've seen him pick up a toy, examine it, consider playing with it, and then chuck it across the room. Seth has a Bert and Ernie fire engine that runs perpetually until the battery goes dead. If it hits a wall, rather than grinding to a stop, it bounces, turns, and keeps rolling. I've never seen Seth actually play with this toy. He brings it into the room, turns it on to make sure it runs, and then takes off to get more toys – leaving me to enjoy the clatterous ambiance.

I go out to the kitchen, expecting to see him enjoying this car, and instead see poor Bert and Ernie, helplessly bouncing off the cupboard doors. Granted, this is how I might expect Ernie to drive, but I find the vehicle's actual operator, Seth, in another room, digging in the toy box.

When I first became a househusband, I tried to ignore the toys all over the house. I altered my method for walking to a sort of long, shuffling stride to save on my feet. But in the middle of the night, when you're stumbling to the kitchen for a drink of water, your feet act like magnets for any cast-iron train engine that got missed during the pick-up.

Incidentally, it always makes me feel better when I step on a toy that makes noise. Seth has a sonic car that makes crashing noises on impact, and that's my favorite one to step on. It makes me feel as though I were exacting some sort of revenge for my throbbing foot.

After several twisted ankles, punctured soles, and stubbed toes, I needed to figure out a way to stop this constant mess. I decided to do some research to determine why a toddler needs to make the house a maze of toys. I started to watch the young entropicite in action.

After careful observation, I confirmed that the majority of Seth's toys are not actually played with. In fact, they seem to exist only to be placed. Seth runs to get them, brings them into the room that we're all in, and then systematically spreads them around. After he observes them in their new place, he runs for more. I'm not sure why, but it seems to be important to take a daily visual inventory of every toy in the house. He must get frustrated himself to find that they get put away occasionally.

One weekend, Lora and I were both sick with the flu, unable to get out of bed, and Seth had free rein to cover the house with toys. Each room had a set of related toys spread out on it, and we were powerless to stop it. I wasn't sure if Seth was marking territory or playing his own house-sized game of "Risk," spreading deadly ankle-breaking toys like little plastic armies. I certainly came away from the weekend wounded.

Through my research, I have also determined that the hands of a child are connected to the brain in a very different way than those of an adult. Every time the thought of a new toy is introduced to Seth, whatever is in his hand at the time is immediately loosed from his grasp and drops to the floor. His motor functions apparently shift from the idea of hanging on to what he's got and start concentrating on what he can get.

My second method of coping with floors full of toys was trying to teach Seth to pick up after himself. However, Seth only wants to help when "Barney" is on TV and singing his "Clean Up" song. Unfortunately, that episode only comes on occasionally, and I refuse to tape "Barney" for any reason, for fear that I might have to see it more often.

With Seth's help a dismal failure, I was left to chase behind the toy-dropping child, picking up the things he left behind. Since he can distribute toys faster than I can put them back, this quickly zapped my energy level. I resorted to straightening up when Seth went down for a nap, but I soon saw the folly in that: I was preparing a clean slate for him to mess up again as soon as he woke up.

It was like what Lora and I do before we throw a party. We voraciously clean the house from top to bottom (like it's never been cleaned before), just so other people can come in and mess it up. Then we have to clean again after they leave. I never understood the logic of that, either.

Finally, I gave in and simply let nature take its course. That's right, entropy. At least, if all the toys are already on the floor, he can't take them out again.

I do pick up the toys after Seth goes to bed, so that the house is orderly overnight. Nobody is able to enjoy it, but at least it's clean for roughly ten hours. During the day, everything is left to tend toward chaos, and Seth is left to tend to it.

Yesterday, I stopped by my buddy John's house to let Seth play with John's two-year-old son, Tom. As John and I reminisced about the old place, I told him that I now subscribe to his theory of entropy in housecleaning.

But, looking around John's house, I noticed that he seems to have changed. His house – and particularly his bedroom – is now neat, orderly, in fact, spotless. (His wife might have something to do with that.)

I felt heartened, however, when we went downstairs to John's family room. Seth and Tom had pulled out every toy that Tom owned, thrown them on the floor, and were standing on the kiddie picnic table, surveying their handiwork.

I guess it's up to the young to test those old theories.

Chapter 9
Buying Nylons

There is no greater test of parenting skill than shopping with a toddler. Every trick you know is needed to make it through a store without a knockdown, drag-out brawl between you and your nineteen-month-old. For a person like me – who hates the whole concept of shopping in the first place – dragging a kid along is a recipe for disaster. Only the crafty, creative, or crazy survive – and that's just the kids. The unsuspecting househusband doesn't have a chance.

Shopping is not a word most men like to say, much less do. For a man – particularly this one – shopping is a necessary evil he has to go through to get things. Not unlike having a tooth drilled to fill the cavity. Where women like to "shop till they drop," for men there are only one-stop shops. If they don't have it there, then it's usually about time for the game to start.

Shopping is tough enough for a househusband even without the kid. What married man hasn't experienced the pleasure of running into the store for his wife to buy a woman's feminine hygiene product and having the cashier yell out for a price check: "Tampons on line one!" But try shopping on a weekday afternoon when you're the only man in the store and you come across "nylons, Misty Taupe, size B" on your shopping list. Such a chore is not for the faint of heart.

First, you have to wander into the women's undergarment

section with your head held high and confident, trying not to slouch so you don't look lecherous. You locate the nylons display and quickly scour the multitudinous names of colored stockings. These range from Black Mist to Mushroom – just what color is that, anyway? – and Nude. (Resist the urge to open that package.) When you finally do locate the Misty Taupe, it's not the right size, so you must continue your awkward and clumsy search.

After about fifteen minutes – with a dozen nylon packages littered on the floor around me – there is no more looking casual at the nylons display. Mothers with children push their carts by, pausing only to cast a disparaging glance. The look seems to say that they don't approve of my kind in their section – especially since I appear ready to open the packages and start rubbing the nylons on my cheek.

And after a couple of sideways looks, I'm prepared to tell anyone who asks that I need these nylons for an upcoming bank robbery, and I'm testing them for an allergic skin reaction.

You put a child into this mix, especially one that has been raised near the warm glow of a cathode ray tube, and every trip to the store becomes a disaster waiting to happen. To kids, cartoons are merely a break between commercials. No matter what they're doing while the TV is on, kids always perk to attention when they hear the commercials. Why, it's only a matter of time before Madison Avenue sets up its own cable network programming: "Ad-TV – All cereal and action-figure commercials, all the time!"

As a result, every shopping trip consists of two opposing forces trying to complete a task together. You have the child who wants everything he sees and the father who only wants the receipt and the way out. The battle lines are drawn, and the vendors are on Seth's side.

Grocery shopping trips usually start out great. Seth is always excited to get out of the house and go somewhere. Since he's not quite old enough to recognize the way to the store, the drive there is exiting and new – father and son out on an adventure together.

Of course, as soon as we pass through the doors and Seth spies the glorious splendor of the grocery store shelves, any male bonding is instantly severed. It's now me against him in a battle of agendas.

Grocers know this is true. Mine brings out the heavy artillery right away: directly across from the shopping cart parking area is the bulk candy aisle. Bags and bins of every kind of candy line the shelves, which are usually decorated in the colors of the season, designed to catch a toddler's eye. You know, it's funny – I didn't know that Veterans Day was a candy-giving holiday.

Wary of this initial salvo, I've learned to grab Seth and put him into the cart before he focuses on his favorite candy. I always position the cart with Seth's back to the candy shelves so we can start shopping before the cart is filled with sweets. My clever maneuver is of no consequence, though, because our grocery store has candy in three other areas – not counting the checkout counter – so I eventually lose that battle anyway.

I used to think that shopping carts were parent-friendly because you put your child in the seat, he faces you, and you can chat with him. Over time, I learned the real reason that shopping carts are parent-friendly: you can see what's coming first and prepare for it. But it doesn't matter – candy is usually shelved at eye level for those in the cart, and a kid can easily grab it as you pass by.

Carts do come in handy at the breakfast cereal aisle, which I try to get through with only three different cereals. Diversion is the name of the game there. I tell Seth that we're a race car and then push the cart fast down the aisle, making Cap'N Crunch, Count Chocula, and the Trix Rabbit all zip by in a blur. I run with the cart until we arrive at the granola and shredded wheat in their boring, adult-colored boxes.

In the cookie section, I push the cart forward and let it go on its own. This gives Seth something to think about besides the Keebler elves – like the possibility of crashing. But I'm always in control, and I always stop the cart just before it runs into the Ho Ho's. This tactic also helps squelch the Teddy-Grahams tantrum that starts at the beginning of the aisle, when Seth turns the corner first and sees them before I do.

(A parent has to come up with some diversion because there is no more pathetic sight than that of a father wrestling bite-sized Oreos from the hands of a little kid, even when the regular and Double Stuff Oreos are already in the cart.)

No method is foolproof, however. A child's hands are quick – especially when he can recognize package labels. I have to be careful never to drive the cart too close to the shelves, or Seth would fill his own shopping list of Pringles, Ritz Bits, Cheetos, and Doritos. And remember – if you must backtrack for a forgotten item, always take the cart with you, or at least park it in the middle of the aisle. You are in for a surprise at the checkout counter or at home if you don't.

When the whining gets out of hand, I have been known to give Seth a piece of candy from one of the open barrels of candy-by-the-pound. Now, tell me, is there a parent alive who has not done that? It not only stops the screaming for the moment, you just might get out of that area without three pounds of orange slice gumdrops.

The only problem with buying a child's silence is trying to tell the checkout person that you'd like to pay for one single piece of candy. One cashier didn't know what to think until I produced the empty wrapper from a butterscotch kiss.

It's not just at the grocery store where a househusband can get in trouble shopping: hardware stores are bad, too. Because I usually don't need a cart at the hardware store, I let Seth roam. And just like any free-range animal, he grabs at everything at his level – and in a hardware store, that means plenty of small, potentially dangerous things. After my first trip there with Seth, I learned why the open containers of nuts and bolts always have mixed-up parts – it's not because of poor shelf stockers.

On a later trip, Seth and I went to the hardware store for a new plastic garbage can and a few other items. Seth sat contentedly in his stroller until we got to the checkout counter.

Right during the middle of the transaction, he demanded to get out. Not paying too much attention to him, I complied. But once he was out, I knew why he wanted to be. Right in front of him was a great big bag of candy corn.

Before I became a parent, I used to think the impulse displays next to checkout counters were for adults like me. It seemed I always found something there I needed. Now, I know it was installed for kids to cajole their parents into buying them something.

Let's be serious, how many times have you gone to the hardware store with a list that reads: rake, garden hoe, nails, 3/8-inch drill bit, candy corn?

Let's be serious, how many times have you gone to the hardware store with a list that reads: rake, garden hoe, nails, 3/8-inch drill-bit, candy corn? There ought to be a law against impulse-shopping counters – and I made the mistake of trying to enforce it.

As Seth screamed, every eye in the place turned to us. The other men in the store seemed to be thinking, "Why don't you tan his little hide once to get his attention?" The woman at the cash register turned a cheek of indifference to me, probably from having heard it too many times – or else she was preparing to ring up the candy corn. I desperately tried to settle Seth down, but he wanted the candy corn and just screamed louder.

Totally frustrated, yet defiant, I picked Seth up and put him in the trash can. He stood there looking at me, dumbfounded, but at least I knew he couldn't go anywhere while I finished my purchase. Whether it satisfied any of the onlookers, I didn't care.

To the slightly shocked cashier, I simply said, "He needs a nap," even though he'd just had one, and then dragged the stroller, my package of hardware, and my kid in a garbage can away from the checkout. I pulled him out of the can as soon as we hit the exit – so that no one outside would think I considered my kid trash – and struggled out the door.

But I had an even worse experience last week at the checkout in the grocery store. There, if you aren't going to let your kid have an impulse item, you'd better let him help unload the cart. A shopping trip is always tiring, so a tantrum constantly lurks nearby. Three people stood in line behind us, tapping their feet and waiting with their few items while our cartload was rung up. The pressure was on, I was too impatient to wait for Seth's help, and he cracked.

With a bawling kid wrapped around one leg and a hundred grocery items to supervise, is it surprising that one tiny little item, lodged down in a corner of the cart, could slip by without me paying for it? I discovered it once I'd gotten out in the parking lot and had finished unloading the groceries and a cranky kid. What was I to do? Should I leave it in the cart for the employees to pick up or should I put it in the car? I sure wasn't going to haul my screaming kid back into the store to pay for it.

As we drove away and headed for home, Seth stopped crying and sat in the back seat, transfixed on me. It's just as well, because I didn't have the time to tend to him. I was having a little trouble seeing where I was going – you never know when a Misty Taupe nylon is going to come in handy.

Chapter 10
Daddy the Healer

Lora apparently made it though childhood without being hurt. She never went to the emergency room, she had no broken bones – I don't think she even knows what an Ace bandage looks like. Heck, she's never even been stung by a bee (and is deathly afraid of them as a result). What can she possibly know about dealing with a small child's pain?

I, on the other hand, am fully qualified. My resume of pain includes small scars like freckles all over my body, a broken wrist, a broken hand, broken fingers, a cracked rib, various sprains, four knee surgeries, and several choking episodes. My parents tell me now that they didn't expect me to live to be older than ten. I am a health care provider's best friend and an insurance company's biggest headache.

Because I know pain so intimately, I figured I should have no trouble taking care of young Seth, who's bound to bump, bruise, and scrape from time to time. At least, that's what I thought when I took over the Doctor Dad job.

Being a combination doctor, triage nurse, and human bandage is definitely one of the stay-at-home parent's responsibilities. Toddlers seem to be always getting sick or injured, usually by blindly walking into something – or stumbling over it. And we expected Seth's physical care to be a fulltime job. When I came home to stay with him, he was coming off a year that held an entire childhood's worth of illness and injury for any normal kid.

When he was five months old, Seth came down with the whooping cough – shortly after he had the second of three shots that should have immunized him against it. It was the Illness from Hell for us. Here we were, cautious first-time parents to begin with, faced with a disease that made our fragile-seeming baby – who couldn't even sit up by himself – shake and turn different colors with violent coughing fits.

We spent the next ten weeks sleeping on the living room floor, with Seth laying between us. Every fifteen minutes, one of us would wake to scoop up a coughing Seth and pound on his back. It made us even more paranoid than the usual new parents.

Because whooping cough weakened Seth's immune system, he spent the next few months fighting colds, flus, and the croup (twice). He had chicken pox for his first Thanksgiving and the flu for his first Christmas. He was in and out of the doctor's office so often in his first year of life that he could have been a poster boy for the health-care system.

On top of all that, when Seth was fifteen months old, he tripped in a hole on the lawn, sprained a knee, and ended up in a plaster cast. By pure chance, this happened on Father's Day, and I spent what should have been "my" day sitting in an emergency room, wondering what was happening to my son.

I think it was the next week that we decided I should quit my job and come home to be with Seth full-time.

I felt reasonably confident that I could handle the physical care of the bumps and bruises Seth would acquire – it was the role of comforter that had me worried. Seth's ill-health had given me ample opportunity to observe the differences between my method of health care and Lora's, and I knew who was a comforter and who was not.

I'm a macho "Pain is our friend" father. When Seth falls down, I laugh in the hopes he will do the same before he decides he's hurt and starts to cry. Lora immediately rushes to pick him up and – given the severity of the injury – might even cry with him.

The differences in men's and women's health-care-giving seem to reflect distinct philosophies. While both parents can apply a Band-Aid, there are definite differences in how it gets there.

A father's first aid consists of chuckling at the mishap and saying, "You fell down, isn't that silly?" His diagnosis is something like, "Aw, it's just a little scrape. You're all right." For treatment, the dad brushes off some dirt, and his prognosis is a tousle of the hair and a shove back into the game.

While both parents can apply a Band-Aid, there are definite differences in how it gets there.

The mother's first aid is an empathetic scream of horror, followed by hugs and kisses, followed by defending her actions to the father: "Well, he fell and hit his knee, for heaven's sake." Her diagnosis consists of firing a lot of questions at both father and son: "Is it broken? Can you walk? Are you okay? Should we take him to the doctor?" Mom's treatment involves washing and dressing the wound, with a prognosis of holding the victim in her arms and rocking him until the cut scabs over.

I think the difference stems from the fact that a man wants his son to handle the pain on his own first – even though Dad secretly hopes it's not real bad. (Now, if it were his daughter who got hurt, that might be a whole different story.) A woman wants to mother the child's feelings first and provide the external care second – and the worse it is, the more mothering is needed. It must have been a man who said, "We have to learn to laugh at our pain."

These differences made for some heated interchanges between Lora and me.

"Don't baby him," I'd say when Seth, who was learning to walk, stumbled over a crack in the driveway.

"He's hurt," she'd respond, as if that justified everything. And then she'd pick Seth up and cover him from me, as if my words added further injury.

When Seth and I were on our own, I quickly learned that my gallows humor wasn't what Seth wanted when he took a tumble – I would need to comfort him, as well.

At first, this was awkward. That first week, Seth came running to me, crying after falling on the backyard patio and expecting to be cuddled in my arms. Seeing a few layers of skin torn from his knee, I tried to look closer and remove any dirt or rocks, but he pulled away quickly, wanting only the healing that a comforting hug could provide.

So I held him for a while, secretly appreciating it – there's nothing like a kid's arms wrapped around you to ease any pain you might have yourself. But shortly, a small alarm went off inside me that seemed to say, "We can't get too mushy here; we're guys, after all."

Reluctantly, I pushed Seth away, mumbling something about my own knee surgeries and scars, something about initiating him to boyhood. As a distraction, it worked, and my sixteen-month-old son toddled away.

That incident caused me to wonder why I couldn't be completely comfortable holding my own son and soothing his pain. Many times I'd seen the unconditional love my wife enveloped him with, healing love pouring out of her body like cleansing water. Why couldn't I just smother him in kisses and stop the hurting, especially since it felt so good to do it?

Deep down, I think, my discomfort came from some innate male responsibility to raise my child to become a man – and the fear that excessive babying from his dad might screw that up. The fact that I was at home in a traditional female role just magnified that fear.

For the next few weeks, I tried my "laugh, it doesn't hurt" response, until Seth – sensing he was missing something – started sticking his hurt fingers and toes right into my mouth to be kissed. I would check in all directions first and then give him a peck on the injured area to make it all better. I couldn't help but feel a little like God, given the almighty healing power of my lips.

Of course, this was always followed by a manly rub of Seth's head, a "You're all right," and a kindly urge back out to play.

But Seth was in the habit of having his hurts kissed, and my less-than enthusiastic compliance didn't always satisfy. Sometimes, he accepted the perfunctory smack from me because he needed validation that he was indeed injured – but then he waited for his mommy to come home for the real healing. Other times, he kissed his owies himself.

I just didn't get it. It took a more dramatic incident to make me understand.

Last Saturday, I was out of the house, helping my brother-in-law move, and Lora had the kid watch. Barry, a young neighbor boy who is Seth's friend, had come to our house to play.

About halfway through the move, I received a phone call from Lora.

"Can you come home?" she said. "The paramedics were just here, and I've got to take Seth to the urgent care center."

While my heart dropped into my shoes, she added, "Seth's okay."

Seth and Barry had been chasing one another through the house, and Seth had tripped on a pillow we kept in front of the hearth (to keep anyone from falling on it) and pitched head-first onto the bricks. Lora, who was at the other end of the house, reached Seth in nearly a single bound. When she picked him up, Seth's face was bathed in blood.

Lora started screaming, Seth started screaming, and Lora raced for the phone. An ambulance and police car were there in minutes. By then, Seth and Lora had both calmed down, and Lora had discovered that only Seth's forehead was cut – and that had already stopped bleeding. Barry's mom came racing across the yard when she saw the ambulance, and Lora had the opportunity to feel embarrassed in front of a lot of people.

(Later, Lora confessed that when she saw all that blood, she thought the top of Seth's head had been sheared off and she panicked. She'd never seen a head injury and didn't know how much even the tiniest one bleeds.)

Lora's story sent me into a tizzy, and I raced to meet her at the urgent care center, where Seth was to be stitched up at the suggestion of the paramedics.

The entire way to the clinic, I cursed out everybody I could think of: myself for not being there, my brother-in-law for moving that day, Barry for not diving and taking the hit for Seth, the driver in front of me for driving the speed limit, and Lora for allowing the accident to happen. I convinced myself that Seth never would have been hurt if I had been there and that now I was needed even more.

When I got to the clinic, I thought, I would take over. Lora had had her sympathetic cry, and now it was time for Doctor Dad to help Seth stoically endure the stitches.

But when I arrived, Seth and Lora were sitting calmly in the waiting room: Seth was playing with some toys, and Lora was reading a magazine, yet watching Seth's every move. The dried blood on his forehead covered a cut that was no more than a quarter-inch long, and everything seemed under control.

Seth was glad to see me, but only because he wanted to play. When we finally got in to see the doctor, the cut had already started to heal, so stitches were useless.

Seth had suffered his worst injury to date, and I had done nothing to help. All I could do was hold him comfortingly while the doctor washed the wound – and to my surprise, that didn't bother him much. He'd already been through the worst part, and Lora, the mother hen, had seen him through it.

So I guess I've learned my lesson about pain and healing and parenting: kids need both parents' styles of coping with pain. It's important to teach your child to endure a little pain because it soon goes away. But for soothing painful owies, there's truly something to be said for a loving caress – and moms are still tops in that department.

And that's all right with this househusband. The next time I have knee surgery, I plan to milk it for everything it's worth.

Part III

Winter

Househusband Axioms

The only place worth dusting is the television screen.

Anything that goes into a child's mouth may not stay there. Half-chewed food can come back out at any time for reasons that include distaste, excess of full capacity, or just because the child wants to look at it.

Bad habits in children are created in threes. The first time Seth came in to sleep in our bed, it was cute; the second time, it was learned behavior; and the third time, he came in with a blanket, a cup of water, and a smile that said, "Where's the party?" After three times, you have to break the habit.

A toddler will never let you wipe his nose with a tissue, especially when he can cuddle up on your lap and drag his nose across your shoulder.

When a kid spits his pacifier out, it always heads directly for the most inconvenient spot to reach and/or the dirtiest spot in the house.

Chapter 11
Seth's Own Agenda

We don't have a life, we have a rough draft!
– A frustrated Lora Oberle, upon coming home from work and finding a messy house and me typing at my computer.

Of course, Lora is right. My transition from reporter to househusband is a constant internal struggle, and I'm never quite polished at either. I clean house only as much as I need to, take care of Seth, and then try to cram in some freelance writing, out of fear that my skills will atrophy. As a result, the house never sparkles and the writing always needs work: a rough draft of a life.

And this is how we limp along from day to day. It's not great, but it's been okay – until I got the phone call.

Don, a former co-worker, called last week to see how I was doing. He had moved on to a new job shortly after I left the newspaper, and he called to check on me and maybe even gloat a little.

"How's diaper duty?" he asked, knowing full well its wonderful pleasures since he has a newborn of his own.

"Oh, fine," I responded, noting his sarcasm. "It seems to be a never-ending cycle. You change one diaper and then get the kid something to eat and drink – in essence, preparing for the next delivery. Kind of like publishing in that respect. Speaking of which, how's your job?"

"It's great," said Don. He's now editor of an international trade magazine, and he proceeded to regale me with highlights of the travelogue he's compiled over the past few months.

"That sounds exciting," I said. "I could use a trip about now."

"Conferences *are* a lot of fun," he said. "You'd enjoy it. In fact, that's why I called. We have an opening in the organization that you might be interested in."

A job!, I thought. Travel, excitement, international fame, and my byline in a four-color glossy (not to mention a paycheck that *I* could bring home). Just the thing I need to get back on the career track – and a move up to boot.

This could be the opportunity Lora and I have been waiting for, our chance to switch places and let Lora be the stay-at-home parent and me be the breadwinner. We set that as our goal when I came home to be the Mister Mom, and now our plan might just be coming true.

How many other job offers am I likely to get? I'm not getting any younger staying at home, and besides, Lora should be home – Lora *wants* to be home. I reasoned that it's easier for a woman to get back into the job market than it is for a man. Many employers seem to cut them some slack when they go off to be a mother for a while. For a man, mid-thirties, balding, and still applying for the same type of position he was in at his last job, a potential employers' thoughts might be more along these lines: "Oh, so you went off to watch your kid for a while. Isn't that nice? Next!"

A chance like this might not come along again. It wasn't the subject matter I wanted to write about, but it was a good job, a well-paying job. It was a great opportunity!

It was wrong.

"You say that you travel a bit. How much travel would there be in this position?" I asked.

"About as much as I do – every few weeks," Don said.

"Do you see much of your family?" I asked.

"No, that's the downside," he answered. "When I go, I'm usually gone for the whole week, and then I have to go back to the office some weekends. I tend to miss my wife and little girl."

I gulped back my enthusiasm. "Thanks," I said, "but no thanks." Lora and I had decided that raising Seth was the most important priority in our life and that our careers should be structured around that – it didn't make sense to take a job where I would be away from my family several times a month. I knew that Lora would be sad but would agree with me.

So I turned down the job – but I couldn't turn off the career thoughts that Don had planted.

Maybe, I thought, it's time for me to step up my freelance writing, to try to write something more than just this diary or the occasional one-page article that I can work on in five-minute increments. Maybe I should call some contacts I have and pitch some more extensive story ideas. Maybe I could become this one-man writing powerhouse, conquering the publishing world from my suburban retreat.

After all, Seth is pretty independent now that he's going on two, and he and I have settled into something resembling a routine: Seth knows how to run the VCR, and I've figured out how to get clean dishes from the dishwasher. Seth hollers when he wants something, and I jump – until I holler back, and then Seth turns up the volume on the TV.

I can put in a videotape and work while he watches it, right? And then there's naptime – a *guaranteed* one-to-two hours of uninterrupted time to make some calls and write stories. Why hadn't I thought of it sooner?

Why? Because nothing is guaranteed with a toddler. No matter what plans I have for Seth – whether for the next minute or the next decade – they won't work unless he goes along with them. I might think that Seth is going to adhere to a set schedule, but he just might have another agenda in mind. And unfortunately, his plans include me the same as mine include him.

For example, little kids crave their parents' attention the

way they crave Kool-Aid, chocolate bars, and any cereal with little marshmallow bits in it. Unfortunately, they want attention at the exact moment they want it – whether or not that's convenient for the parent. And they don't hesitate to let you know when you're not giving them enough.

Two days ago, I decided to get some serious writing in, convinced that Seth was occupied with his pack of scooters, trikes, and baby-four-wheelers. I got so involved with my work I didn't notice that he had lined up all of his bikes around the foot of my desk. When he was finished, he walked into another room and called to me. I got up to see him and did a flip that only Dick Van Dyke could appreciate, nearly killing myself on a Big Wheel. Was this a trap set by my son to get my attention? If so, it worked.

Yes, every kid has his own agenda – and a parent probably isn't going to be able to change it. Seth, for instance, likes to play with water. One day, I was in the kitchen, cleaning up a glass of water he'd purposely spilled (his favorite game), and he stood watching me, another water glass in his hand.

"Seth," I said, "if you do that again, you'll get a time-out."

Seth looked at me and then at the glass. Then, with a small smile, he turned the glass upside down and watched the contents cascade onto the floor. Before I could say a word, he took off running, straight to his time-out chair. He sat there, grinning at me.

That little son-of-a-gun had weighed the consequences and gone for it anyway.

When kids learn how to talk, it helps you understand how their little minds work – but that may not be what you want. What parent, for example, can get used to their son using the word "penis" (even though that *is* its name). When Seth first discovered his penis, it began with a touch, followed by him saying "Fun," and then giggling. How do you respond to that?

As a fellow male, I had to resist telling him that he was on to something. Instead, I said, "That's your penis. It's time to put your diaper on now."

But Seth doesn't need any language to tell me he doesn't like my writing – grunting and pulling my fingers off the keyboard works just fine. He also knows that when Daddy is on the phone working, anything in the cupboards or refrigerator is his for the whining. It's not a good idea to be screaming at your kid when you're talking to the editor of the local parenting publication about a story idea on creative discipline for toddlers.

So I'm going back to doing most of my writing at night or during naptime – *if* Seth takes a nap, that is. Seth doesn't like to sleep at any time of the day or night, and some of our biggest battles stem from my determination to follow a strict nap schedule versus his desire to personally witness every bit of daylight in his life.

Some of our biggest battles stem from my determination to follow a strict nap schedule versus his desire to personally witness every bit of daylight in his life.

Why does a child fight so hard to stay out of bed in the afternoon, just so he can spend it alternating between whiny tantrums and zombie-like stares, all the while muttering his mantra, "Don't wanna take a nap"?

Seth is an angel when he's sleeping, but he's crafty as the devil to avoid getting there. When naptime arrives – and he's tired but doesn't want to sleep – he tears about the house, begging for one more tape, one more book, one more glass of water, and brimming with crazed laughter as he escapes my grasp. "Dad," he seems to be saying, "it might be on *your* agenda, but it ain't on mine."

And as my window of writing opportunity gets eaten away by his maddening playfulness, my patience as a father slips away with it.

Sometimes, I get mad at him for taking away my time,

and I don't lovingly put him to sleep. In fact, I yell. Then I have to rock with him in the rocking chair, trying to settle him down. As I hold him, I notice a hole inside me, created by anger, where love should be pouring out, but it's not. It's usually there, this feeling of connection formed by heart pressed against heart, with love moving from one to the other. But when you're tired, mad, and late for a deadline, there's only a void.

Yet the amazing thing is: if you rock with him long enough, his love hole starts pouring back into you, and you both relax. I might miss an opportunity to write, but what the heck.

It's moments like these when I remember what's important. Conquering the publishing world can wait – a small child is not going to fall asleep with anger, only with love. When is the last time you've been screamed to sleep by anyone? (Not counting that AC/DC concert when you passed out before intermission.)

People are always arguing about whether genetics or environment has a greater effect on a child. But it doesn't really matter – after conception, environment is all we have left. Yelling at the child to force him to follow your agenda or constantly ignoring him for your own needs will have the greatest effect of all. I *will* keep writing when I have time, but not at the expense of Seth.

You see, life is always a rough draft when you're raising kids because they're growing and changing everyday. Each day, you get to perform that magic juggling act: his agenda versus yours. As a parent, you can't throw out the rough draft and start over. You can try to refine the product, but you're never going to achieve perfection.

And once you're a parent, you don't get a chance to change your career. You're a parent everyday and always, and everything else is a second job.

Chapter 12
Spinning Yarns

Cocktail parties are hell for the househusband. After all, at a cocktail party, you're only worth talking to as long as you appear interesting. Once the novelty of the status wears off, a Mister Mom quickly becomes a secondary character in the discussion, struggling to get a word in edgewise. Believe me, when vying for the conversational spotlight among a crowd of lawyers, accountants, and businessmen, it's best for a househusband to act like a doctor – a spin doctor, that is.

Saturday night, Lora and I attended the annual Christmas party for my circle of college friends. I hadn't seen a lot of these guys since the previous Christmas. At first, when talking to them, I played it straight, earnestly explaining that I was staying home taking care of my son, that this was a privilege and a decision Lora and I had made, and so on. That usually earned me a moment of awkward silence, and then the topic of conversation switched – more often than not, to their latest achievement.

"Hey, Joe, I hear you're staying home now," Mike, an old friend from my college dorm, sidled up beside me.

"Yeah . . . ," I began.

"That's great," he jumped in. "You know, my wife's doing that. She quit her job after I won that big case last year. You remember that case, it was . . ."

After a couple of comparisons with wives, I scurried for

cover with Mike's wife – anyone's wife – anyone in a maternity outfit. I found a group of housewives and quickly donned my family man persona.

"I was making Seth some pizza recently," I began. "You know, that's his favorite meal. When the oven timer went off, I said 'Seth, pizza.' His face lit up, and he immediately took off running. I followed him to the front door, where he jumped up and down yelling 'Pizza.' I guess we have pizza delivered a little too often."

The family man persona is useful when talking to sympathetic stay-at-home females. They know what a chore housework and child care are, and they're more than happy to talk about it all evening long. But they also know the joys of finding something good on daytime TV, the bliss of spending summer days outside, and the secret, if not guilty, pleasure of taking an afternoon nap while the kid is doing the same.

For a good hour, while my buddies stood around the keg rehashing the latest Vikings loss, I held the attention of the party's homemakers by telling housecleaning horror stories, commiserating on how difficult it is to stay home, and tossing in a cute kid tale every once in a while. I had found my audience. I was one of them.

But soon, my party Eden was disrupted. A working mom joined us, her interest piqued by talk of my situation. Suddenly, the tone of the conversation changed. Gone was the easy familiarity we had shared, the sense of being an insider. In its place was a kind of . . . wariness.

"You're staying at home?" she asked, as if just discovering that my kind actually exists beyond the pages of magazines. "How's that going?"

"Oh, it's okay," I replied, trying not to sound as though I really like it. "But it's a lot of work. With the housework, cleaning and changing the kid, meals and laundry, my days are full. It seems like I need to get a babysitter if I want to get any writing done."

"Uh huh," she said and sauntered confidently away.

I had instinctively changed to the martyr persona – it always works well with the working mother. Reciting the litany of daily chores and bemoaning the dreariness and lack of coffee breaks makes them feel great about their decision to work.

You see, announcing that you've quit your job to stay at home and raise your kid can be tantamount to announcing you've joined the wrong political party, or at least uttered something politically incorrect – regardless of whether you're a man or a woman. Not everyone believes that I'm doing the right thing by being a househusband. Some people respond as though they're not going to say anything because they can't say it nicely.

A staunchly feminist friend later joined our little group and grilled me about househusbandry.

"What's it like to be a Mister Mom?" she asked.

"Oh, it's a full-time job," I said, offering a flash of the martyr routine, so she could enjoy seeing a man in his rightful place. "Anyone who thought that child care is not work, has never done it."

"So, you'd rather be working and have your wife stay home with the kids?" She tried to trap me.

"Well, I liked working for the newspaper, but Lora and I decided it was important to have someone home with Seth," I said. "We're both equal partners, and one of us had to sacrifice their career. I was glad to do it."

"That's right," she interjected. "It's about time women had a turn at the career track."

"She also made more money than I did," I added – which brought a smile to her face, because I had just validated the existence of the women's movement.

The discussion then turned into a debate of the merits of day care versus stay-at-home child care, and I left it. The women, with beers in their hands, were beginning to resemble a female version of the Miller Lite "Tastes great - Less filling" commercials. You know: "Less stress - More fulfilling."

I mustered up the courage to join a group of old buddies again. I chose guys who come home on the weekends to rut around the house, bursting into the full flower of manhood with power tools and dirt. With this crew, you have to be ready for anything.

"Joe, what are you doing now?" asked one buddy.

"I'm at home taking care of the kid," I answered, courageously.

"You're not working?" he replied in amazement.

"I'm between jobs right now," I said, "but I am freelancing – you know how it goes."

"Oh, yeah, the economy. It's hitting everybody."

"Yeah, it sure is," I replied, without lying.

"So what do you do all day, watch sports on TV?" asked another of my friends.

"Well, Seth likes hockey, so we've caught a few games this winter," I answered, still unsure where this cross-examination was leading.

"Man, I wish I had that kind of time," he said. "I could finish off the basement rec room."

Now, first of all, this guy has no idea how a twenty-one-month-old behaves around electric power tools, nor does he realize that sheetrock screws feel real good when rubbed on teething gums. He wouldn't have hung one wall before he'd given up in frustration, grabbed an ice-cold beer and sat down with the kid in front of regional trap-shoot competition reruns on ESPN. But the idea in cocktail party conversations is to go with the flow.

"I know what you mean," I replied. "We redecorated three rooms this summer and are making plans for doing our basement." What I didn't tell him is that our 'redecorating' consisted of simply wallpapering, and even *that* we hired out.

I did make sure to tell my buddies that my spare moments are spent looking for work, leaving little time for writing. Somehow, I knew that complaints about the time-consuming task of child-rearing – the story that works well with mothers – would fall on deaf ears here. "Give the kid a hotdog out of the fridge, chase him off to bed and tell the wife 'he didn't need changing until you got home, honey,'" is this crew's idea of child care.

Instead, I gave a frustrated and downcast look, shook my head, and cussed the economy, staring ahead with a pall that said this situation has been thrust upon me, rather than of my own design.

At the end of the evening, I found myself in a mixed group of people – career-climbing husbands, working wives, stay-at-home mothers, and what-have-you. Not knowing who to please with what slant on my situation, I fell back on the only remaining recourse I have: self-deprecating humor.

"It's not such a bad deal," I babbled. "Househusbands even have their own role model – Mister Rogers, you know, from 'Mister Rogers' Neighborhood.' Here's a guy who spends his afternoons sitting around his house until the mailman arrives. Soon, he's off visiting other people's places of employment and asking them about what they do. When he gets back to his house, we hope to find out exactly what he does all day, but he avoids it by spinning some fantastic yarn about going to the 'Land of Make-Believe.' "

Only Lora, who was standing nearby, did not laugh.

So I survived that Christmas party with my career dignity intact. But last night, we were at a Christmas gathering of my wife's family, and I had to go through it all over again. Unfortunately, none of the personas I'd adopted at my friend's party work with my in-laws. Few words carry any weight with my father-in-law, other than, "I'm still looking, sir."

Chapter 13
I Can't Believe I Have Dishpan Hands

As a kid, I hated to do dishes. I alternated weekly dishes duty with my brothers and sisters, and it was the bane of my existence. While I wiped the dishes my mom washed, I would look out the backyard window at the neighborhood kids playing and plead: "Am I done yet?"

Once I nearly severed my middle finger by wiping a just-sharpened butcher knife. I loved it because I got to skip a turn in the rotation. My older brother said I did it on purpose, but I thought I deserved more time off. If only a little blood could excuse me now.

The household chores you despised as a kid change when they become your regular duties as an adult. No one else is there to do them, so you just accept them and do them yourself, sometimes even taking pride in their completion. This is how I've come to look at my duties as a househusband – although I didn't reach that point easily.

I went through three stages of development in my relationship to housework: denial that I actually had to do it; acceptance, coupled with marginal performance; and excellence – trying to be the best househusband I could be.

In the first stage, I stalled by telling Lora that I didn't even belong in the kitchen – I've got an old construction-job injury to my back that seems to bother me only when I'm stooped over the sink scouring pots and pans. Lora was not sympathetic.

But my personal discomfort is the least of it. I'm a danger to the kitchen and probably to anyone that comes near me when I'm cooking or cleaning.

I once dropped a hot stove rack on the vinyl kitchen floor, branding it for perpetuity. I set Seth's red popsicle on the butcherblock counter for later and forgot about it – and then cleaned the stain with a scouring pad. I slice vegetables without a cutting board, leaving notches on the countertop and dining room table.

One time, I started a fire in a pan by letting oil burn too long. My first reaction was to put the fire out with a towel. When the towel started on fire, I took the pan to the sink and put water in it, making the fire bigger. When I carried the pan back to the stove to cover it with a lid, I sloshed some oil on the floor and started another fire there.

I half expected to see Oliver Hardy standing near me, smacking me on the head with his hat. Of course, then I could have used it to cover the fire in the pan.

I didn't fare much better with the laundry. I couldn't use my college-days method of hauling the clothes home to my mom on the weekends. And as a bachelor, I had done my laundry in one load, whether I waited a week or a month.

So when I took over the clothes-washing duty at our house, Lora feared for her white clothes. For several months, she wouldn't let me near them.

I certainly didn't deserve this level of paranoia. So what if I've turned white shirts green and pink, reduced sweaters to unidentifiable baggy garments, washed wrinkles *in*to clothes, and lost legions of Seth's little socks (but never in pairs). For some reason, my own wash always turns out fine – perhaps because it all turned to one color long ago.

However, as time wore on – and Lora's time became limited – I was forced to take over her clothes as well.

No big deal, laundry is easy: put the clothes in the washer, pour the soap in and turn it on, right? Wrong. Apparently, women's and children's clothes are made differently than men's.

According to Lora, clothes have to be sorted into like colors. A launderer has to turn shirts and sweatshirts inside out so the lettering or designs won't be destroyed. Kids' clothes must be presoaked because toddlers like to wear their meals before they eat them. (Incidently, you can always tell whether your young kid is right- or left-handed by which sleeve is covered with more food.) All of this dramatically increases the time spent doing laundry.

Lora also insisted that I empty all pockets before throwing pants in the washer. She didn't want her clothes to have little white paper speckles like those stuck to mine after I ran a load through with used tissues in my pants pockets. Every time I did my wash, the laundry room looked like ants had thrown a ticker-tape parade.

> I half expected to see Oliver Hardy standing near me, smacking me on the head with his hat. Of course, then I could have used it to cover the fire in the pan.

I cavalierly laughed at Lora's suggestion to put her underclothes in small mesh bags because I didn't want the extra work. If it can't be tossed into the machine with a minimal amount of handling, I don't want to do it. As a result, I probably have the record for the most busted bras and ripped underwear – outside the bedroom.

Other household chores I felt confident I could handle – mainly because I didn't do them. Toys spread around the house stayed that way until after Seth went to bed. Scouring the bathtub was unnecessary; the shower curtain, if I remembered to close it, hid the tub. And any piece of food stuck in the carpet that couldn't be sucked up by a vacuum cleaner was probably stuck there for good.

As for dusting – well, that was my sisters' job when we

were kids, so I never learned how to do it. Besides, dust always forms an even pattern, and if you don't disturb it, you never know you need to dust. So I prefer to just leave it alone. I plead guilty to being dusting-impaired.

And then there's diapers. The only thing I can compare changing diapers to is when I was working at a soybean manufacturing plant one summer as part of a crew that was ripping down the old parts of the plant. We cut apart the old pipes that used to carry the soybean meal – it now had rotted inside them after several years of nonuse. My job was to get rid of the rotten meal that poured onto the ground.

I would stand by and silently pray the pipes would be dry and empty when the steamfitter cut them open, but they usually held a little surprise. It was a crapshoot as to which color meal flowed out of the pipe, as well as the smell that went with it. Yellow was relatively okay, because it was still the color of soybeans and probably had only been there a few years (a blink of the eye in rotting-soybeans time). White was bad because it meant the concoction had started to break down; it tended to singe my nose hairs. And black was the worst because it had probably been rotting for decades; the smell caused me to long for summers on my uncle's farm, shoveling manure. The only way to stop smelling the stuff was to remove it, and the only person to do it was me.

Changing diapers is similar. I hope the diaper is high and dry, with no surprises until the kid's mother is home. But the smell usually forces my hand, so I pray for a normal color because some are certainly more odoriferous than others. Then as now, I have no choice other than to clean it up.

And just as the chore of diaper-changing became mine, at some point, I started to become more comfortable with other household chores, as well. I stopped battling the impulse to reject housework as beneath me and decided to do a good job at it. While the time of the change is unclear, the manifestations of it have been plain to see.

First off, I agreed with Lora to do the laundry according

to her instructions (except for mine – hey, no need to mess up a good thing). I began to pride myself on how many loads I could do in a day. And I started to clean the lint trap on the dryer in a timely manner, actually enjoying the act of peeling the entire layer off in one motion. When I told Lora of this simple pleasure, she looked at me as if the laundry room walls should be padded.

At the dining room table I became a dynamo, quickly finishing my meal and racing to the sink to start the dishes. In college, I had a rule that nobody was allowed to get up from the table and do dishes immediately after a meal – it must be done later, after we've digested our food (thus alleviating my guilt at not wanting to do it myself). But now, if the condiments and used dishes were not cleared away by the time Lora was done eating, I started to lose it and sat in my chair fidgeting at each passing minute.

I got to the point where I couldn't rest until everything was done. If housework was my job, I decided, it was going to be done well and on time.

"Relax a bit," said Lora, used to a more leisurely dining experience. "You know, I heard some woman on the radio say that she was having real trouble in her marriage because her husband nearly takes things out of her hand at the table."

I acknowledged her point and gave her back the catsup bottle.

But I had turned a corner in my career as a househusband. My dad had always told me to do my job well, no matter what it was, and to leave it like a man. Well, while I might feel more like a man leaving housework than doing it, it was my job regardless, and I planned to heed his advice. I assumed Lora's comments were just jealousy toward my newfound prowess.

I did the job well, too, until last Friday evening when I was furiously trying to clean the house for the weekend. I was planning to watch an NFL playoff game and wanted to do it with a clear conscience and a clean house.

I had washed every stitch of clothing not in use, cleaned and vacuumed the house, clothed and fed Seth (and Lora, for that matter) three times, and was just finishing the supper dishes. Seth had been particularly dependent and incontinent all day, which made my job tougher and my nerves all the more frazzled. Still, I unwaveringly kept my eyes on the prize, which these days is a clean, comfortable home I can be proud of.

As I was wiping down the sink after the last dish had been done and the dishwater drained, Lora waltzed into the kitchen. She pulled a plastic cup from the cupboard and filled it with water. Innocently relating Seth's latest cute trick, she drank a few swallows, poured out the rest, and then set the cup next to the sink.

I believe she had left the kitchen by the time I blew – perhaps she didn't even see the steam emanating from my ears. But it didn't matter: she had done nothing wrong. She was merely thirsty and had gotten herself a drink. It was me that needed correcting.

When I settled down and analyzed my problem, I realized that as a journalist, I've always experienced closure. You write a story, it's published, and then it's history. You move on to the next one. Barring nasty letters or troublesome libel suits, no story ever requires effort after it's finished. The same, unfortunately, can't be said about housework.

The drudgery of housework continues ad infinitum, no matter how well you do it. Even while I'm finishing a chore, the next one is already preparing itself. While I do dishes, the rest of the family is eating; while I do laundry, they sit around dirtying their clothes; while I vacuum one room, the other rooms are filling up with dry skin.

And of course, Seth's digestive tract doesn't have a pause button.

In the end, though admirable, my diligence is somewhat dubious – fame in housework is fleeting. While a clean house is nice for the moment, it's a matter of "What have you done for me lately?" Pursuing excellence in household chores is futile, because they never are done.

I now know what every housewife who ever strapped on

an apron knows. And all I have is one question, for anyone who will answer:

"Am I done yet?"

Chapter 14
Puppy Movie

Television is a necessary evil for a parent. For the beleaguered househusband, it grants precious minutes of freedom by grabbing and holding captive the child's undivided attention. Anyone with kids who doesn't think that the electronic babysitter is an essential parenting tool has never wanted to go to the bathroom by himself.

Lora and I are members of the first generation to grow up with the warm blue light constantly humming in our subconscious, so we know full well the joys and danger of television. In fact, we're full-blown addicts. Before we were married, Lora and I had one of those Serious Discussions: we would not, we decided, allow television to become a dominant force in our future children's lives.

"I'll build a stand to keep the TV set up high," I vowed, "out of reach of the kids."

"And I'll limit their viewing time," Lora pledged. "I'll give them all sorts of playtime options and teach them to turn the set off and do something else."

It was a solemn moment, to be commemorated in only one way: I reached over, grabbed the remote control, and turned the channel.

So we were doomed from the start. It was not a good sign that Seth and I watched hockey on TV together the day after he was born. Seth lay on my lap quietly as I twisted and turned with the action. At the time, I figured his silent interest indicated he would become a hockey player someday. I now believe that he was thinking of the players on the tube as a crude Sega-Genesis video game.

By the time Seth had been home from the hospital for two months, he was already plugged in. "Cheers" had been our nightly viewing fare while Lora was pregnant, and no matter where Seth's infant seat was in the room when he heard the words, "Sometimes you want to go/where everybody knows your name," he would crane his neck to see the TV. I've heard that babies can recognize voices while in the womb, but who would have thought they'd be memorizing TV theme songs in vitro?

When Seth contracted whooping cough at five months and woke with coughing fits in the middle of the night, it probably didn't help his TV habit any that I rocked him back to sleep in front of CNN News. Lora, however, preferred the blue-grey light of Nickelodeon re-runs when she woke to nurse him in the middle of the night. She later confessed to hoping he'd wake up at three a.m. for a feeding so she could catch "Dobie Gillis," which she'd never seen in its first incarnation.

When Seth was still less than a year old and in his walker, he liked to wheel to within an inch of the TV set and reach his arms up to it. We joked that he was worshipping at his own electronic altar, but we didn't know how right we were.

The battle over the tube has been extremely difficult to fight given that we, as parents, haven't taken the cure and rid ourselves of our boob-tube addiction. Our house itself is on the other side in this war – it's armed with five TV's and three VCR's. (Since Lora and I married later in life, we had each amassed our own small electronics arsenal before joining them together.)

We had also already established some deeply ingrained bad habits and an extreme lack of will power. And when I became the househusband, the temptation to indoctrinate my son into the wide world of televised sports was impossible to resist. I found myself on the front line in the electronic drug wars, and I was already a junkie.

Here is my war diary:

When I first came home to be a full-time dad, I didn't think that TV would be a problem right away. Seth was only sixteen months old, after all. Not old enough (so I told myself) to be affected by the brightly moving shapes on the box in the corner of the family room. I would have plenty of time before I had to worry about his TV habits – and plenty of sports to watch in the meantime.

But Lora warned me, the further gone of us two addicts, that I should curb my viewing habits before Seth was old enough to copy them. Do something besides watch TV all day, she said – and I'm still not sure if she was talking about me or Seth.

Now, I had sworn off soap operas years ago. And Oprah, Phil, and Geraldo – with topics like "Transvestites and the Clothiers Who Love Them" – didn't seem appropriate viewing for a couple of guys at home together. But I figured that public TV was okay for Seth, and "Sesame Street," "Mister Rogers' Neighborhood," and "Reading Rainbow" soon became our daytime staples.

I'm not sure what Seth thought about it all, but I quickly got hooked on the antics of Thomas and the other engines on "Shining Time Station." "Sesame Street" was always good for a laugh and an occasional Hollywood celebrity cameo. I even started relating the goings-on in Mister Rogers' Land of Make-Believe to Lora at lunchtime.

To demonstrate some restraint, I tried to talk Seth out of watching "Barney." It's not a real sacrifice on my part, though, because more than two minutes of Barney's voice is enough to make my skin crawl. Lora didn't buy into my protestations of martyrdom.

Neither one of us was too concerned about Seth's TV-watching yet. On the practical side, we both recognized that the TV kept him busy and allowed me time to get things done around the house (when the shows were in reruns, that is). But on top of that, we were both convinced the children's programs on PBS were actually good for our growing toddler. Seth was learning something from the shows, and Lora was there to witness it.

It happened one September day when Lora came home for lunch. She found Seth standing in front of the tube watching "Sesame Street." Grover was singing an alphabet song, and as Lora reached out to hug Seth, he started to sing along. Transfixed, we both just stood there and watched our eighteen-month-old son recite the alphabet, using his best possible pronunciation.

When the song was over, we started to quiz him to find out just how many letters he knew. Grabbing a nearby magazine, we pointed out A's, B's, and C's, asking him, "What's this?" He knew every one.

While I was tempted to take credit for Seth's academic growth, I knew better. TV was the third parent in our house, the one in charge of teaching and learning. And with football, hockey, and basketball season upon us, I didn't want to rock the boat. It would be the perfect opportunity to quiz Seth on his numbers – jersey numbers, halftime scores, and yardage, that is. In time, I figured, Seth would be ready to challenge me in "Jeopardy!" – he already liked to dance to the Final Jeopardy theme song.

Of course, there's always too much of a good thing, and this fall Seth discovered afternoon cartoons, all fortified with at least eight important commercials. Before I realized what had happened, Seth's brain pan was filling up with advertising logos, jingles, and slogans faster than you could say, "I'm cuckoo for Cocoa Puffs!"

Seth is a testament to the power of TV advertising. For example, he loves pizza and gravitates to the TV whenever he hears a pizza commercial jingle. ("Call 488-8888. Pizza Hut delivery is really great.")

We learned just how strong this power was in December. We were driving to my sister's house when we pulled up at a stoplight and waited. All of a sudden, from the backseat Seth started pointing out the car window and howling "Pizza! Pizza!" We looked and, sure enough, across the street was a Domino's

Pizza store with its bright red-and-blue logo. In just a few short months, TV has created trademark awareness in our son.

We figured this had to stop. It was pizza logos now, but with all the sports I watch, it couldn't be long before we would be driving with Seth's grandparents past a bar and he would shout, "Daddy, this Bud for me?"

Our problem is that we still thought we had control over this habit we'd created. In fact, rather than turn the TV off or restrict Seth's viewing back to commercial-less public TV, we decided to buy videotapes. This ushered in a whole new era in television viewing at our house.

(I'd like it to be stated for the record that Lora bought Seth his first videotape. She came home one day shortly before Christmas with Walt Disney's *101 Dalmatians*. At last count, 101 is about how many cartoon tapes we now own.)

Seth was obsessed with the Dalmatians tape. He wanted to watch it every day – he requested it in the morning as soon as he woke up and used it to bargain for more time before he went down for a nap and in the evening before bed.

"Puppies! Puppies!" was his battle cry, and I grew disappointed when this great cartoon movie from my childhood began to usurp the morning PBS viewing I had come to enjoy. I began to lose track of new visitors to the Land of Make-Believe and had to resort to playing with Seth's toy Thomas the Tank Engine myself when I needed a little "Shining Time Station" fix.

The Puppy movie became a daily ritual around our house, which quickly brought about limited viewing. I would even cajole Seth into watching "Barney" rather than back-to-back Dalmatian screenings.

Lora and I have seen the show so many times that we can discuss it like film scholars might scrutinize *Citizen Kane*.

"I see something new every time we watch it," I told Lora one evening.

"I know what you mean," she replied, sitting up in her chair. "You can see strange formations in Cruella De Vil's smoke."

"You're right," I said. "She has to be the most politically

incorrect cartoon character ever. She worships furs, she smokes in every scene and is a terrible driver to boot. I wouldn't be surprised if she didn't have a little something to drink before she got behind the wheel."

"Why does it seem like Disney always has a female villain in his cartoons?" she began.

"Aha," I said, jumping in to counter her point. "So you think Walt Disney was a misogynist then?"

And so on.

Part of the attraction that the Dalmatians movie has for Seth must be the puppy named Lucky. Lucky is always propped in front of the TV and needs to be torn away from it each night. Seth must identify deeply with this character.

Finally, enough was enough. We had to do something about the Dalmatians film festival held in our living room each day. So what did we do? We bought more videotapes.

The next tapes Lora brought home were Mickey Mouse, Goofy, and Donald Duck cartoons. Because they were shorter, we thought that would cut down on the hours logged in front of the TV. Unfortunately, the shorter tapes just had to be repeated more often, which hastened the point of adult burnout.

Then, Lora bought another full-length feature, Disney's *Beauty and the Beast*. (How lucky for us to be raising our child at a time when Disney is putting all their movies out on videotape – because we'll eventually buy them all.)

Just what we're creating finally began to sink in a couple of weeks ago after an early evening viewing of that Oscar-nominated classic. Seth had been particularly concerned about the scene when the Beast saves Belle from a pack of wolves. As we tucked him into bed, he struggled mightily to tell us something. In his first multi-word sentence, he asked, "Puppy eat guy?"

We assured Seth that the Beast was fine, but we began to wonder what exactly our kid is getting out of all this tube-time.

I've always justified Seth's watching a little TV during the day because it allows me time to do necessary things – like take a shower. But now I began to get visions of someday sharing my couch with a pot-bellied, unmarried, unemployed, cartoon-addict thirty-four-year-old son, and I got scared. It was time to turn the TV off.

Unfortunately, by this tender age, Seth has already mastered the controls to both the TV and the VCR, and he doesn't really care what I have to say about it. Things have gotten out of hand.

It's so bad that I've actually had to explain the difference between cable and antenna TV to our toddler. Seth wants to watch the shows he likes wherever the little portable set will go. Why, he wants to know, won't Mommy's little hand-held TV air the Mickey Mouse cartoon that is playing on the family-room TV – how is he supposed to eat supper so far away from his two-dimensional friends?

For a distraction, I tried letting Seth watch our home movies of him. From this, I discovered something new altogether. The real-life Seth laughs at the things the video Seth laughed at and screams in sympathy with the Seth on camera. The real Seth answers the filmed questions much more quickly than the on-camera Seth ever did. He even started asking for the home movies, referring to the Seth on TV as Seth in the third-person – "Watch Seth tape."

When I heard that, I just stared at my young son, dumbfounded by the realization that he is living out the McLuhan-esque axiom that says that nothing is real unless it happens on television.

At that point, I'm ashamed to say that I gave up trying to cut back on his TV viewing. I rationalized that the trade-off of time to myself is worth it. Besides, if Seth is going to throw a fit every time I say no TV, we won't have much fun playing together. I'll try to entice him with alternatives before he remembers the TV each day and to make sure that what he does watch is decent. No murder and mayhem, sex or violence, and no MTV, especially "Beavis and Butthead." Okay, he can watch "Ren and Stimpy," but only when his mother isn't around.

Yesterday afternoon I was writing, and Seth had just gotten up from his nap. The TV wasn't on yet, but I wanted to finish what I was doing so I mentally conceded that it was only a matter of time before I would need to turn it on.

"Pochio! Pochio!" Seth yelled, coming up to me and pulling on my leg. This is his way of asking for the tape of Walt Disney's *Pinocchio.*

"You can watch it," I said, "but I have to work."

I got up from my chair to find the tape and the remote control, but then I noticed he had stopped asking for the tape and was sitting with his Pinocchio book, paging through it. He stopped at pages and laughed like I'd never heard him laugh at the movie.

I sat down with him, and he asked me about the pictures, laughing and enjoying the version in the book. And suddenly it struck me – it was *me* who wanted to turn the TV on and not him at all.

My son's problem with TV is really my problem. I hadn't realized before this just how strong my hand has been in creating this little TV-aholic. The power the medium has over him is actually the power I have over him and changing it is indeed up to me.

It's clear to me that if I want to create a real boy rather than one connected by video wires to the TV, it's going to take more than wishing on a star that he turns out right.

What the heck, the house might stay dirty a little longer, but TV has already claimed one victim in this home. I'm determined not to let it claim any more.

Chapter 15
Hair Wars

Lora and I have never seen Seth's scalp. Not that we've been looking for it for any particular reason. It's just that he was born with such a healthy shock of dark brown hair that we've never seen what the top of his head looks like. Given all the other intimate physical details we know about him, it's interesting to think that we haven't seen this most traditionally public of baby places.

Seth had such a head of hair, in fact, that a nurse spotted it in the womb during his final ultrasound appointment. We left the doctor's office not knowing the sex of our baby, but by God, we knew it had hair. The kid's mane made him the Samson of the hospital nursery, and when it comes to haircut time, he's always been as protective of his locks as that hirsute Biblical character.

The hair wars started early in our house – as soon as Seth was born – but initially they were fought between Lora and me. I argued that a boy's haircut should follow a simple philosophy: once it starts to look shaggy, you cut it as short as possible, so that you don't have to cut it again so soon. Saves time, saves money. Very efficient.

Lora's response was less philosophic and more of an anguished cry, "You're not cutting all the hair off of my precious baby!"

For the first several months of Seth's life, his baby-fine

hair grew in little wisps, while Lora harbored visions of curly-locked infants and I tried to tell her that our child didn't look like that. Then it came time for Seth's first photo shoot. After one look at the proofs of the unshorn six-month-old tyke, she quickly agreed that a trim was in order.

The proofs (which have been squirreled away for future embarrassment during Seth's cocky and defiant teenage years) lowered the term "having a bad hair day" to a new level. His bangs had gone to seed and were curling like a bad moustache at one side of his forehead, while uneven growth on the sides and a wild ducktail sticking out from the back completed the look. It was not unlike the multi-style coiffures many of today's adolescents are paying money to have.

We decided to take Seth to an expert in cutting children's hair – his grandmother. As a newborn, I, too, was blessed with a thick thatch of hair, and my mom first cut it when I was at the tender age of three months. (She waited that long, she later told me, because it covered the odd shape of my head.) Over the years, she gave me and my two brothers many butch haircuts, occasionally experimenting with a mohawk style prior to cutting it all off. Once, in a truly avant garde mood, she even taped my ears back, which she now claims was at my request.

So my mom was unfazed when faced with a seventeen-pound client. Coolly and methodically, she trimmed Seth's hair in a conventional style approved by the nervously onlooking Lora. Seth fidgeted no more than any six-month-old made to sit still for twenty minutes while patches of itchy hair slipped down the back of his shirt. The haircut and the subsequently re-taken photos were a complete success.

Now, whether Seth detected the confidence of years of haircutting experience in my mom's fingers or whether he simply felt safe in her ancestral hands, I don't know, but over the next year-and-a-half, no one has been able to tearlessly come near his head with a pair of shears other than my mom. The only problem is that Mom's Hair Salon is located ninety miles south of our home. With other haircutting options just down the street, the trip is hard to justify.

At first, we timed visits to my folks' home with Seth's hair growth, and my mom always kindly obliged. But we knew this wouldn't work forever. Finally, when Seth was a year old, Lora broke down and took him to a beauty salon with her. She reported relative success – the novelty of the situation must have interested him.

> Over the years, my mom gave me and my two brothers many butch haircuts, occasionally experimenting with a mohawk style prior to cutting it all off.

When I became a Mister Mom, Seth's hair care fell into my domain. The first time I took the sixteen-month-old Seth for a haircut, I took him to the local eight-dollar haircutting salon, and, following Lora's advice, I placed him in my lap. It didn't go as well as Lora had always reported. The stylist *was* able to cut Seth's hair, but only after a lot of pleading and cajoling, plenty of fidgeting, a few tears, and the consumption by Seth of quite a few hair-covered Bearwiches cookies. I gave her a big tip and told myself there had to be a better way.

The next time, I added myself to the haircut list, hoping that sitting on my lap and watching his dad manfully submit to the shears might help Seth accept the situation. The only thing it did was increase the amount of hair that irritated his neck.

Seth's resistance to the idea of haircuts increased dramatically with each one until even trying to comb his hair became a small battle. I pleaded with Lora to let the barber give him a butch, hoping that by the time it grew back he would have forgotten his dislike for the procedure. Lora, the self-ordained arbiter of the haircuts, would not give in.

By this time, Seth was more than twenty months old, and I was putting him in my lap so that I could physically hold him still while the stylist tried to do her job and the other customers eyed us in aggravation. But the stylist's reticence was catchy, and I finally threw in the towel with half of Seth's head trimmed at best. The stylist charged me half price – I doubled it out of embarrassment and vowed as I left that this had to stop.

Luckily, my mom and dad came for a visit a week later. I put Seth in his chair at the dining-room table, set up the TV and VCR on the table in front of him, popped in his favorite tape, drove up a legion of toy cars and trucks, and remained on hand for further distraction detail. My mom finished Seth's haircut without incident.

I surmised that TV must be the answer. When it came time for Seth's next haircut, I tried one more trip to the stylists – although I did head to a new salon across town, hoping my son's reputation hadn't traveled that far. This time I brought our small, four-inch TV along to distract Seth. The television reception was somewhat fuzzy, and this drew unhappy whines out of him. I feared for the worst.

I began batting the TV antennae, trying to bring in Bert and Ernie more clearly. Then I drove Seth's toy Thomas the Tank Engine up and down the barber chair, crashing him into my legs in hopes of getting a laugh. Heck, I would have drawn blood if I figured that would have helped.

Nothing worked. Seth yelled every time I spoke and recoiled from each snip of the scissors. I corralled him like a human straight-jacket, trying my best to immobilize his head, and the stylist raced around the chair, clipping here and there as if she were trying to cut the colors off a spinning top.

Hair salons are full of mirrors, so no one escaped the torturous sight of Seth screaming on my lap. But I was determined to finish this haircut (we weren't planning to see my mom for a while). By the time it was over, Seth and I both needed a bath to get the hair off, and my wallet took another beating. I was extremely flustered and in a hurry to leave, and I sternly urged Seth to "C'mon."

Still in tears, Seth incredulously – and courageously – pulled me back toward the chair, the scene of the indignities he'd suffered. With his hair-covered pacifier hanging in his mouth, he mumbled something urgent and pointed to the TV I'd forgotten. The look on his face seemed to say, "You may be able to cut my hair, but you can't have my TV."

Since we didn't get a whole lot of hair taken off, I could already see the next haircut on the horizon. Fed up, I bought a pair of barber scissors, called my mom for a few pointers, and mentally prepared for what I fully expected to be the mother of all haircuts.

I pulled out all the stops for my haircutting debut on my almost two-year-old son: the clearest TV in the house, the most recent VCR tape, the sweetest cookies, and every toy truck, train, car, block, or ball I'd seen Seth take interest in over the past few months. With his senses sufficiently overloaded, I grabbed a handful of hair and started cutting.

Seth sat still. It seemed as if he didn't know I was there. Like my mom suggested, I ran his hair through my fingers and cut what was above them, thinning out the back and top. I worked as fast as I could, occasionally miscutting here or taking too much out there. But progress bolstered my confidence, and I quickly cut his bangs before he knew what was going on.

The bangs were uneven, so I tried to correct them, and Seth brushed my hands away with a warning whine. I went back to thinning the top and back, where I felt safe, like a timid swimmer scurrying back to the beach when a wave comes in. Besides, there were plenty of mistakes to correct there, as well. We resumed an uneasy truce, and I was able to carve a small peak into his neckline. I figured that my luck was running out, so I had to move on. It was time to trim the sides, and experience told me this would be the hard part.

Unfortunately for Seth, he was born with a pair of ears like mine, which are nearly big enough to pick up satellite transmissions. This size of ears attracts the sharp metal of barber scissors, and I got them both. The first ear only received a scratch, made when Seth squirmed as I tried to trim above it. But it made cutting around the other ear all the more difficult, and I drew blood on that one. Tears from the first ear turned into anger on the second, and the haircut came to a screeching halt. Any cutting from this point on would have required a good wrestling hold or several shots of strong whiskey.

After soaking up the droplets of blood and comforting the wounded, I surveyed the damage of the first haircut I'd ever given. The longer I looked (and the more I combed) the more satisfied I became. I could see the mistakes – the slanted bangs, the tails in the back – and I wanted to fix them. But I also knew that we'd reached some sort of middle ground, from which it was best not to wander. I decided to let the memory of sore ears fade.

As I cleaned up the hair, I felt a feeling that I never anticipated: I couldn't wait to do it again. Compared to the agony at the hair salon, this haircut was a breeze. But it was more than that. The more I cut, the better I seemed to get at it, and – until the bloodletting – the more I enjoyed it. I actually feel anxious for his hair to grow back so that I can perfect the mistakes I made. Just think of all the stress I can prevent Seth from going through, all the money I can save. And all the different haircuts I can try: bowl cut, butch, mohawk . . .

I wonder if Seth prefers masking tape or cellophane tape on his ears?

Part IV
Spring

Househusband Hints

Vacuum tracks in the carpet are not unsightly – they're a sure sign to your wife that you've vacuumed.

The best clothes to dress a kid in are cute little bib overalls because you can carry the kid like a sixpack. It leaves the other hand free . . . for carrying a sixpack.

Don't ever eat the last cookie, cracker, or piece of candy in a bag that the child might have known existed before he went down for a nap – unless you have another bag on hand, that is.

Despite what your wife might say, using the vacuum cleaner to clean the spice rack is okay – it's the closest thing to a power tool that a househusband gets to use.

Always use a sunblock of 50 or higher – unless you want your wife to know what you do during the day.

Chapter 16
Other People's Kids

As the saying goes: you can choose your friends, but not your relatives. Well, if you have kids, you may not have any choice in the friends, either.

Seth has made "friends" – as much as a two-year-old can – with some kids in the neighborhood. This forces me to interact with their parents – in effect, choosing friends for me. Normally, this would be fine: as neighbors, we have natural contact. But like everything else, my lot as a househusband throws a kink in the works. Not all of the parents of Seth's buddies seem willing to choose me.

But I'm getting ahead of myself. First, let me talk about Seth's buddies. The neighborhood kids re-entered our lives this spring. Like bear cubs wandering out of the den, they wandered into our yard, looking for whatever is new in their world since the big winter hibernation. And since Seth is two now, old enough to play with, he's of interest.

Unfortunately, there are only a few kids in our neighborhood, and they're all significantly older than Seth. Joey and Johnny live on one side of us, Travis and Trevor live on the other, and Barry lives behind us. Joey and Johnny show a genuine interest in Seth, but Travis and Trevor are another story. Upon entering our house for the first time, Travis and Trevor brushed past Seth, marched into our family room, and surveyed Seth's toys with the air of an appraiser. Apparently, they decided that Seth's toys weren't good enough, because they then went into the kitchen and opened the refrigerator to survey our food.

Since all of these kids have a couple of years, a few inches, and quite a few pounds on Seth, having a Mister Mom in his corner gives Seth a distinct advantage for once.

Take last Saturday, for example. Travis and Trevor came over for a visit with their mom. I was using an industrial adhesive to replace the carpeting on our front step as they pulled up on their bikes. The boys' mother chatted away while I worked and the boys worked at aggravating me.

"What are you doing?" Travis and Trevor chorused. Not waiting for an answer, they began picking up the glue can and tugging at the carpet that was drying on the step.

"That glue's not going to be easy to get off," I warned, loud enough for their mother – who would eventually be saddled with the cleaning chore – to hear through her own chatting.

"Stop that," she said absently, but her mild chastisement served only to increase the pestering.

Finally, Seth spotted the boys from inside the house and came outside to join the fun. This attracted the pair into the front yard, where they began "playing" with Seth. Unfortunately for Seth, being the smallest, he was the playee in this "game," which most closely resembled the political handling of a Third-World country by two superpowers: you can stand up just long enough to almost gain your balance before we push you down again.

The first time it happened, I thought, "They're just playing." The second time, I thought, "The old man can't protect you from everything." The third time, I intervened.

As little Kremlin and the White House prepared for another attack, I raised my voice. "Hey!" I said, in an attempt to alert their mother to the situation. Apparently she had seen it before in her own house and didn't even look up.

"Stop that," she said, but the tone of her voice didn't even warrant an exclamation point – kind of like absent-mindedly shooing a fly that's just buzzing nearby.

When Seth hit the dirt again – not sure whether to laugh or cry – I told the boys to come over and check out the glue. Secretly, I wanted to use it to glue their hands together. Unfortunately, by now they had lost interest in me, far too busy with easier prey.

I all but forgot about my work, wondering how to handle this situation while not appearing as either a doting father hen or a raging middle linebacker ready to knock the pair of them across the street. Fortunately, at this point Lora came outside. She engaged the boys' mother in mid-sentence, so I invited all three kids out back to play in Seth's new sandbox.

When we got in the backyard, well out of earshot, I interrupted Seth's cordial invitation to come into his sandbox.

"Listen, you two," I said in my best Dick Butkis voice, grabbing both boys by the arm. "You had better not push my kid down again or there'll be big trouble with me. Seth is younger than you and can't defend himself against big kids like you. You have to take it easy."

Their eyes began to widen as I described how I would defend my son, so I eased up and told them to play nice with each other.

At the moment, Joey and Johnny arrived and were instantly set upon by Travis and Trevor. The four of them chased around the yard, knocking each other down, struggling to their feet only to run around again – with Seth running a few steps behind in unknowing laughter. It was just like any initiation I ever witnessed on "Wild Kingdom."

I decided that as the only adult I had better step in and settle the troops. But just as I was making my move, the aggression settled on its own. In a moment, Joey and Johnny asked Travis and Trevor over to their house, and they were gone. I was left with Seth, wondering exactly what happened.

My first thoughts were of relief: the rough boys had been lured away from my vulnerable two-year-old son. But as I watched Seth eye Joey and Johnny's house from his empty sandbox, I started to think that maybe I was wrong. Granted, Seth is still too young to battle five- and six-year-olds, but he still has to find his own way. Who am I to choose his friends for him? Not every kid is looking to take him out – they just have different ways of getting to know each other.

While most of the neighborhood kids get bored playing with the younger Seth, Barry genuinely has fun with him. Barry is a prince of a kid – he recognizes the age difference between him and Seth, and is very good at putting up with it. Of course, he has a special reason for being so careful – Seth's dad is always watching.

Barry is a great friend for Seth. I loved having him around, until one day a couple of weeks ago when he started talking about his own dad.

Seth and I were playing ball in the backyard when Barry tooled up on his brand-new bike. Seth immediately quit playing ball and began admiring the vehicle, while Barry proudly sat down with me to chew the fat.

"My dad thinks you're a jerk," Barry said, quite matter-of-factly.

"What did you say?" I replied, slightly stunned.

"My dad thinks you're a jerk," Barry said again. "My mom doesn't think so, and I know you're not a jerk."

"What did I do to your dad? Why does he think I'm a jerk?" I demanded to know. I had never even met the man.

"I don't know," Barry replied, sheepishly. "He said, 'Why does that jerk have to grill out all the time?'"

Now that I knew why, I was even more confused. Barry's dad thought I was a jerk because I cooked food on my grill? Why, grilling out is practically a necessity after a long, hard Minnesota winter. At least he could have met and talked with me before branding me a jerk – I'd be willing to allow him that opinion, then.

I questioned Barry as much as you can a five-year-old, but he could offer nothing more. It was one of those offhand remarks that people make and kids repeat, without either one thinking about it, but it began to gnaw at me. I feel like the neighborhood oddity as it is, but I don't want other, gainfully employed fathers to agree.

The more I thought about it, the more paranoid I became. After all, Barry's folks have a grill sitting in their own backyard – they never use it, of course – but still, grilling couldn't be the real reason. It had to be something else.

I wanted to ask Barry's mother about it the next time she collected her kid from my house, but I didn't want to let on that Barry had broken his father's confidence – assuming that his father even cared. I could only sit and wonder about it.

Two days ago was the first time I saw Barry's father set foot outside the door. I still had no clue why the grilling bothered him – I've never seen him shake a fist at me from his window while I grilled my supper. Is it the smell? Is he barbecue-impaired and jealous of my charcoal-flavored burgers? My firing the grill up for Johnsonville Brats certainly doesn't attract people and noise the way they do on the TV commercials. What is so terrible about someone grilling outside?

My househusband's guilt could leave me with only one conclusion – Barry's dad has seen me spending valuable workday hours sitting in the warm springtime sun with Seth. He must perceive me as a lazy father who spends his days playing in the backyard and grilling on the patio rather than toiling behind a desk for some grumpy boss. Here I am, unemployed, and audaciously having a good time at it.

Barry's dad began mowing the lawn; Seth and I were relaxing on the back steps with some popsicles. I decided to bring this non-relationship to a head, so on his next pass I raised my hand in greeting. This startled Barry's dad.

He had been looking at me from across the yard, and now, when I waved, he nearly steered out of his mowing pattern. It was a friendly wave, so he was forced to acknowledge it, and he did, with a stern, one-swoop forward motion. To me, that one motion translated into: "Aw, go on, get off your dead rear and get a job. What kind of man are you to let your wife work? I hope the sun fries your sissy-white skin, like the meat you cook on that damn grill."

He never looked my way again, so I decided to rescind my olive branch. I try not to let it bother me, because I have a new problem: Barry keeps coming over when we're about to eat. One evening, I was sending Barry home because it was Seth's supper time. Frustrated that his play time with Seth had been cut short, Barry said, "Why don't you ever let me eat over at your house?"

Now, if the truth be known, Barry eats constantly when he's at our house. I have to cut him off so Seth doesn't spoil his supper. But his request was a good idea, so I asked him to stay.

"What are you having?" Barry asked.

"Tacos," I replied.

"Ick," he said, "I don't like meat."

I went through a litany of menu choices and finally determined that Kraft macaroni and cheese is the only food he likes. Since I only serve that at lunch time, I told him we'd do it another day.

Barry and I have played this little menu game many times over the past few days. I pull everything down from the cupboards and out of the refrigerator to try to please Barry, while Seth tugs at my shirt, begging me to let him stay. Exasperated, I finally broke down and told Barry I'd make macaroni and cheese.

"Are you sure it's okay with your dad," I asked, "if you eat over here?"

"Oh," Barry replied, "my dad won't mind."

"Good," I said. "It will give me a chance to try out a new recipe."

"What is it?" asked Barry.

"It's called barbecue macaroni," I said. "Fresh off the grill."

Chapter 17
My Mom, Myself

For Mother's Day, I sent my mom a card that read: "Thanks, Mom, for putting up with me all those years. You did my laundry, cooked me meals and cleaned up my messes . . . and still found time to play with me and comfort me when I got hurt." My mom, a stay-at-home parent herself, rarely got thanked for her efforts, so I'm doing it now, with a Hallmark card.

As I sealed the envelope and pondered my next chore for the day, it occurred to me that my mental duty list reads exactly like that card. And in an instant, my greatest horror hit me like a load of damp laundry:

I'm turning into my mom.

It wasn't supposed to be this way. I was supposed to put off, as long as possible, acting (and looking, for that matter) like my old man. And then when I got married, had kids, and finally started to mature, I would realize he wasn't such a bad guy and that it might not be so bad to be like him.

But, instead, my role as househusband has created in me a different animal altogether. While maintaining my God-given male physical characteristics, I've started to act and sound like my mom. This kind of thing is okay for my sisters, who've been moms-in-training all their lives. But for me, a rough-and-tumble, sports-loving, formerly hard-nosed reporter trying to hold onto his machismo while wearing an apron, it's a devastating realization.

I guess I should have seen it coming – the signs are everywhere. First, and scariest, are the things that I say lately.

"Wipe your feet. I just cleaned that floor," I told Lora when she came home from work.

"I don't talk just to hear myself," I told Seth after the third time I called him for lunch.

"Sit in that chair right, or you're going to fall and break your neck," I said once I got him to the table.

These sayings come out of nowhere, obviously burned into my subconscious from having heard them so many times when I was a kid. I find myself wondering if I don't need to pay royalties or at least somehow attribute the quotes.

Another sign is that the smallest things bother me. For instance, Lora needs a new glass when switching from milk to water during a meal. Doesn't she realize that rinsing out the one glass saves on dishes? Then, there's the peanut butter issue. Lora doesn't like creamy peanut butter, but it's the only kind Seth can eat. Creamy peanut butter is the same thing as chunky-style – but without the chunks – yet Lora insists that I buy both kinds. She also insists that Seth wear clean pajamas to bed every night, even when he's played in the sand box all day.

These are trivial things that only a mother – and now her son – would notice. But little by little, they add up to more work for the houseperson.

I must have committed equally grievous errors for my mom. I remember playing in the backyard as a preschooler, digging in the dirt and staining my shorts in the grass, while only a few feet away, my mom was hanging her fourth load of wash on the line. The sun kept me warm from the breeze, but it beat hot and unwavering on her sweaty brow. I was innocent, yet unconscionable – I could at least have sat on a blanket and not wiped my hands on my shirt. Mom, she just washed another load.

Even as a young adult, I didn't get it. Mom used to say that her house is like a hotel: people stop in for meals and a bed, and then they're gone.

At the time, I thought she was kidding, but now I know she was right. I'd hitchhike home from college late Saturday afternoons, check in, eat dinner, and go out for the evening. On Sunday mornings, I'd roll out of bed in time for Mass and come home to a big spread on the table. After lunch, it was into the den for Vikings football with Dad and my brothers. By the time the game was over, my wash was done and packed for me to head back to school.

Mom was right: a house can seem like a hotel to a house-person. I just didn't realize that the guests started checking in so soon.

Mom was right – a house can seem like a hotel to a houseperson. I just didn't realize that the guests started checking in so soon. Seth doesn't hitchhike, but he orders food and drink while engrossed in "Sesame Street" like the most self-absorbed college student. And what am I going to say to this two-year-old, "Get it yourself?"

Yet another sign of my mom-ness is more subtle, but no less telling. At our Easter potluck gathering at my in-laws' house, my mother-in-law took our dish-to-pass from Lora and then turned to me. "Does it need to be heated up?" she asked – but I hadn't prepared it.

So, my in-laws have accepted my new role – or are at least going out of their way to act like it.

Even worse is Lora's and my own blind acceptance of my metamorphosis. During Seth's birthday party, held at our house, I was busy preparing the meal while Lora hustled down into the basement to haul a card table and set of chairs upstairs. (Gloria Steinem, eat your heart out.) As I grated a chunk of my thumb into the shredded cheese and then put a Sesame Street bandage on it, I couldn't help but recognize the incident as a microcosm of my current life.

Although I didn't realize it at the time, nobody can say

you are your mom better than your mom herself. Shortly after Easter, we were at my parents' home. I sat at their kitchen table, beer in hand, and launched into a tirade on the trials of keeping house – a typical ruse I use to divert my parents' attention away from the fact that I'm not employed.

"I can't believe how much work it is to use a dishwasher," I complained. "Lora won't let me put plastic in the dishwasher because it might melt. Wood-handled utensils can get ruined, and it might even scratch our brand-new stainless steel pots. I end up washing loads of dishes by hand, anyway!"

Mom was silent, preparing supper through all of this. Finally, she turned and said to me, "My, what an old housewife you've become."

Beer came spurting through my nose. Everyone laughed, but she had hit on a vein of truth. Later, Lora expressed concern about being married to an old housewife, much less her mother-in-law. I had no reply.

After mailing Mom my card, I tossed all these memories around in my head until Mother's Day, when I gave her a call. It doesn't help my feelings of disorientation much that she's now holding down a job. (So, is she turning into me?)

Mom asked me how Seth was, and I asked her about work. She talked about the politics of dealing with her co-workers, while I complained about changing Seth's diapers, getting him to eat and take a nap. We exchanged advice.

As we talked, I realized that Mom really likes her work, despite its problems, and doesn't seem to miss the difficulty in raising five kids. Since she devoted nearly thirty years of her life solely to raising us, I figured that was the pinnacle for her. Yet you'd almost think that she didn't like it, the way she turned to paid employment at the first opportunity. When I look at her now and see how she enjoys her job, I almost feel like we were holding her back.

But she never made us feel that way when we were kids. Whatever she was doing for us at the time always seemed like the most important thing to be doing – my mom never made us feel like we were a chore.

When I hung up the phone, Seth ran by with an open cup of water in his hand. As Seth and I made a game out of cleaning up the spill, it occurred to me that my mom was a pretty good guy to be.

But if anyone tries sending me a Mother's Day card . . .

Chapter 18
Splendor in the Grass

I knew I'd reached adulthood when I finally began to enjoy working outside. Mowing, shoveling, and raking – the jobs I was forced to do as a child – became simple pleasures, a short diversion from the sedentary headwork of writing.

And when I became a househusband, chores outside became an oasis, a respite from the unending cycle of diapers, laundry, and dishes. The jobs that my parents used to yell at me to do, I now wait anxiously to perform. And spring is loaded with yardwork chores.

At the first sign of greening in the backyard, I decided to check out the lawnmower. As I left the kitchen, I announced loudly to Lora and Seth that "I am going to the garage," so everyone in earshot would know I was going to be a dad for a while. I wanted to be the first on my block to cut the grass, just in case any of my neighbors silently questioned who ran the power tools in my family.

I moved the cars out of the garage and surveyed my space. Since it's my second spring in this house, I felt welcome as an old friend in the garage – even though it had been since last fall that I'd spent any time there.

After a quick inspection of the mower blade (sure enough, it was still attached), I took a trip to the gas station to buy gas and oil. I poked around the spring lawn care section for a while, acting like I knew what I was doing, and then I purchased a cigar to smoke while I mowed, something I had seen a neighbor do. Besides, a cigar gets soggy if you smoke it while you are doing dishes.

I returned home with my supplies, gallons of testosterone coursing through my veins. As I turned the corner to my street, my heaving chest caved in like a backyard sinkhole – the entire block was filled with rakers, weeders, seeders, and waterers. I suddenly felt very far behind and way in over my head.

None of my neighbors was mowing, however. Being a relatively new, slightly insecure suburban homeowner, I decided to follow their cue. Besides, they all have actual lawns, and the pasture-like plot of straw we purchased from the previous owner is in much need of attention.

As to my late start, I asked myself how many of these guys had made breakfast and dressed a screaming kid before they got outside. I'm sure they were having a leisurely cup of coffee and exchanging jibes with the neighborhood seed dealer while I was changing diapers. As a househusband, I muttered to myself, I have more to do with my weekends than just yardwork.

No matter. So I wasn't the first out in his yard – I was out there, nonetheless. I had separated temporarily from the kitchen and was amongst the yardmen of my block, sharing an annual bond like the borders of our properties share the color green.

Except that my yard wasn't exactly green – it was more like a pale yellow, where it wasn't brown dirt patches. Only viewed from the perspective of a bug in the grass did the lawn resemble anything that needed to be cut. So I found a rake in the garage and started digging up the dead thatch, pulling what remained of the sod with it.

As I rutted away, shaking dirt from the withered sod roots of my lawn, Stan, my slightly slope-shouldered and nicotine-mellowed neighbor, left his seeder and sauntered over with a look of bemusement on his face.

"Wha'cha got, Joe?" he asked, as if the disease in my yard were covering my body.

"I'm not sure," I replied. "There's dead patches of grass all over. I don't think the last sodding took here. Did the previous owner resod during a drought?"

"I don't know," said Stan. "But I had that same stuff last year. It's gone now."

"How did you get rid of it?," I asked, wondering why he had asked if he already knew what it was.

Stan took a drag off his cigarette, cast a glance sideways, and leaned toward me like he was about to utter a state secret. I half-expected him to produce some contraband grass DNA enhancer out of his inside jacket pocket, but instead he whispered something that sounded like "everything but lawn-icide." It immediately sent up a red flag.

> "Wha'cha got, Joe?" he asked, as if the disease in my yard were covering my body.

"Oh, we're trying to go organic here – for the kid and all," I said, "That stuff sounds like it's got some chemicals in it."

Stan was taken slightly aback.

"Well, of course, it's got chemicals in it," he laughed. "You're not gonna get rid of that crap without them. I'll go get it and show you."

As Stan ambled back to his garage, I continued my organic lawncare, digging and scratching like a hungry chicken. Lora and I had agreed that we don't know which chemicals are safe – and we aren't sure the manufacturers do either – so we decided it's best not to use any. We want our kid to be able to play in the yard without fear of growing a third arm.

Lora is the most strident in this resolve, yet I agree. Who knows what this stuff does to a growing child's system, I thought. I want to have grandchildren some day – as long as I don't have to stay home with them, that is.

Stan meandered back with half a bag of the herbicide and a promise that it would clear my yard's complexion right up. I said I'd check it out at the store, but he called my bluff and offered the bag to me. I declined, and then we debated organic versus chemical weed control for a while, with me throwing in my kid's health as a defense and Stan anxiously puffing on another cigarette.

"Heck," I said, quoting how the father of Hall of Fame baseball player Harmon Killebrew once responded to his wife's complaint about the worn patches in their lawn, "We're raising kids, not grass."

Stan, toxin in his hand, pressed harder and harder, like a bad influence on a playground, until I uttered the one phrase a househusband should never say.

"There's really nothing I can do about it," I said, "my wife is dead set against it."

Stan couldn't answer. Several rejoinders started to stumble across his lips.

"Your wife?" he said. "What the hell does she know about . . .? Who does the yard . . .? This stuff's not going to hurt anyone. It just drains into the ground."

Finally, he said the only thing he could say and remain a concerned and welcome neighbor.

"Well, suit yourself. But you won't get rid of that crap without it."

"You may be right," I yelled to him as he retreated across the street. "We'll have to see. Thanks, anyway."

Stan hasn't been back to discuss lawncare since then. But that's okay – I have only so much time between meal preparation to flex my agrarian muscles.

I dug up the worst spots in the lawn, backfilled some holes, seeded the whole lawn, and prayed for rain. I must have prayed too well, however, because once the rain started, it didn't stop for a month. But don't get me wrong – I prayed for just a little rain. Besides, I was alone when I prayed, so if anyone tries to pin the flood of the century on me, there were no witnesses and I would deny it in court.

While May held few bright spots, weather-wise, my lawn got just what it needed. I still can't claim to be a member of the

Two-Hundred-Blade Club (you know, two hundred blades of grass per one square inch), but the new grass that sprouted has covered the dead spots, like a few hair plugs on a balding man. Stan was right, I didn't get rid of the "crap," but at least it's hidden. Green is now the dominant color in my backyard, and the border lines are harder to determine.

All that grass has lead to plenty of time behind the power mower, which, for the ego-drained househusband, is just what the doctor of psychiatry ordered. Mowing gives me a lot of time to think; unfortunately, what my stir-crazy mind tends to think about is . . . mowing.

It occurred to me immediately that, to my neighbors, mowing is more of a vocation than a diversion. Mowing interested me as a kid, but only until I mastered it, then it became a chore. I mow the lawn like I cut my hair: cut it short until it grows back and then cut it again. My neighbors, however, take the job to new levels, literally.

One neighbor must have tractor tires on his mower, because every time he cuts his grass, it's only shorn to the length of my lawn when it's time for me to mow. He mows twice as often as I do and cuts only a fraction of the grass. I wondered if he doesn't just vacuum the grass, the suction laying it over to one side and giving the impression that it's been cut. Of course, the guy doesn't have any kids.

Another neighbor must be in training for the big leagues of lawn care because he alternates the mowing pattern in his yard – he mows diagonally, cutting the opposite way with each swath, for that professional baseball outfield effect. Just once, I would like to see him allow the neighborhood kids to play a ballgame and wear basepaths into his lawn. I'd sell peanuts and hotdogs for that.

But nothing says lawn obsession like watering, especially during the worst flood in a hundred years. It was well into June before we went three days without a rainstorm, but on that third day, the sprinklers were spraying, bringing liquid refreshment to the parched and thirsty grass of my neighbors.

At least one neighbor can't help it. He learned lawn care from his dad, who used to place small plastic cups around his lot when he sprinkled, making sure each corner of the quarter-acre received the same amount of moisture. Apparently, the son must need to water like a dog needs to, well . . . water. I can see that I wasn't raised right.

I became scared for my own lawn care inadequacies. In fact, the more I mowed and pondered the greener grass on the other side of the line, the more I wondered what they thought of mine. I became convinced that my neighbors hated my lawn and that they blamed it on my being a househusband.

Then, one day I was at the neighbor's house directly behind ours, and I could see my lawn from the perspective of his dining room window. I sheepishly apologized for the blighted grass, saying that I inherited some problems from the previous owner. To my surprise, he tried to tell me it wasn't that bad.

"I hardly ever notice," he said.

I realized then that the neighbors must secretly like to see my lawn dead and yellowed – it makes theirs look all the better by comparison. Things couldn't have been better for them: the lazy, inert previous owner had been replaced by a feeble, agriculturally-challenged househusband.

It finally began to sink in – Joe's lawn is the control subject in this blockwide lawn-growing experiment. Joe's lawn demonstrated what, if left unattended, the conditions of the area could do to a lawn. His lawn is what could be, while theirs are what *can* be.

I began to notice everything. Since we have no fences in our neighborhood, borders are drawn by where my neighbors spray weedkiller and I don't. And not all of the borders line up: since I moved in, the neighbors on my flanks have carved a generous swath out of each side of my lawn. One neighbor conveniently mowed so the telephone pole between our lots is located on my property.

It's all a big chess game, only the board is green and the game pieces are Toros, Snappers, and Weedeaters. I figured I could start a border war by one mismow of my lawn, but I thought I'd better not. Considering the attention these people pay to their lawns, I knew I would be treading a dangerous area – they have chemicals, after all.

Finally, it happened. I was mowing after dinner last week, while Lora was with Seth inside the house. As I passed the sliding glass door, Seth was standing there looking for me to come by. He mouthed a kiss to me through the glass and when I returned it, he replied with his latest act for people who try to kiss him: a child's version of a bronx cheer.

Having heard it before, I recognized it, but seeing it mimicked through the glass while the mower roared was too much for me, and I laughed out loud just as I was cutting the border between my lawn and my neighbor's.

I had no idea that I'd swerved into his grass until my mower started bogging down from the thickness of his lawn. As quickly as possible, I moved the mower back onto my property. Then I stopped to look back and saw a patch of grass cut from his yard approximately ten feet long and half a mower wide. I looked at his house to see if I was being watched, but saw no one in the windows. I looked back at Seth, and he was still laughing.

There didn't appear to be anyone home next door, so I tried to quickly correct my mistake. Mowing more of my neighbor's lawn to smooth out the jagged cut, I found that each "fix" required a little more cutting farther on – at this rate, I would soon be mowing his whole yard. Out of fear of destroying any hidden water cups, I decided to cut my losses rather than any more of his lawn.

After surveying the damage, I quickly retreated to my house, concerned that I would be seen examining the edge of my lawn. As I did the supper dishes, I watched from the window for when the neighbors came home. Thankfully, the sun had fallen before they did, and I hoped the grass might grow back before they noticed it.

Over the weekend, I heard the mower roaring next door, and I peeked out the window to see what was happening. I half-expected to see my neighbor packing a shotgun on the side of his riding mower, since I was sure he would trot out all his power to demonstrate who had squatter's rights. So I had to rub my eyes when I looked, because coming around the side of the house was his wife, pushing a mower over the disputed province of our lawns.

This was even worse than I expected. What was meant by this gesture? Where was my male rival in this battle of yard wars? Where was the riding mower, loaded down with toxic chemicals to keep me at my distance? Was he afraid of my aggressive mowing, frightened from his mower by my colonial-like yardwork? What point was he trying to make by sending his wife out to do his battles?

I watched her as she carved out the borders around her property (clearly reclaiming the lawn that I had captured on my mismow). She went around twice for good measure, with the mower height at a lower setting, more closely resembling mine. Then she criss-crossed the lawn, mowing diagonally for that ballyard effect – just to show me she was a bad-ass, I figured.

Upon finishing the mowing, she strapped on the weedeater like it was a rocket launcher and chewed up every stray blade in the lawn. She bagged up her clippings, slung them over her shoulder, and dumped them with vigor into the garbage can. Then she wiped her hands clean of the yard dirt and went inside.

I was done in. This guy's wife made my yardwork look like I had been playing in the sand. Apparently, he sub-contracts his "light work" to his wife. I was left with only three choices: retreat, make peace, or counterattack. As any good househusband would, I walked into the kitchen, grabbed the dishtowel from Lora, handed her a cigar, and told her the lawn could use a trim.

Chapter 19
Daddy's Little Secrets

Lora sits at work wishing she were home, so I've learned to take some precautions. There are some nice benefits to this househusband job, starting with sunny afternoons in the park, lounging around the backyard wading pool, and sprawling in front of the TV when you're too tired to do anything else. And since I want to keep the benefits, I try to control what Mommy knows. This includes keeping secret some of the good parts and making sure she knows all of the worst parts of staying home with the kid. Any househusband worth his salt needs to learn this delicate art.

Sleep is an important benefit. I've trained Seth to go to bed somewhere between nine and ten p.m.; as a result, he usually doesn't wake up until after nine in the morning. Ostensibly, this is for Lora's benefit. When she leaves for work, he's still asleep, but when she comes home, he's full of energy and ready to play for the next few hours.

However, this arrangement also works well for me. Secure in the knowledge that Seth will sleep until nine, I can stay up late and watch David Letterman, a rented movie, or anything I've taped during prime time that Lora won't let Seth watch (which is pretty much everything). This is my down time, my alone time, which I need for my sanity. Of course, Lora doesn't appreciate the fact that I'm still in bed, too, when she leaves for work.

Naps also get taken around our house – and not only by Seth. As a canny househusband, I've learned to speak in a normal voice immediately upon being awakened by Lora on the phone, should I be caught napping – literally.

"Oh no, honey, I was just concentrating deeply on this freelance story."

A cordless phone is essential for the surreptitious househusband. If you keep the phone next to the couch when you doze off, you can let it ring twice while you slap yourself awake, clear your throat, and warm up your voice. If you have to let it ring four times while you trip and stumble across the room, your wife will know you've been napping and the late-night movie rentals will become a thing of the past.

I finally learned to tell Lora, "Don't call during naptime." I just didn't add "particularly mine."

I've also become a "Jeopardy!" fanatic during the time I've been a househusband. I pretty much got the okay on "Jeopardy!". (I told Lora that the questions keep my writerly mind sharp and are a good source for at-home research.) But I need a quick finger on the mute-button of the remote if Lora calls when MTV is on. There will be no MTV Summer Beach Party for Lora's son, much less the kid's old man.

"No, honey, that's not MTV, that's just the weather channel. I'm trying to see if I should take him outside. Yeah, I know that it looks nice out, but I just want to be sure."

I've also caught up on my reading as a househusband. Newspaper reading is okay, because Lora usually thumbs through it before going to work. So I'm basically free to read it cover to cover while Seth lounges in front of "Sesame Street" in pajamas until ten o'clock. I just have to race around making sure that he's fed breakfast and changed before Lora gets home for lunch, and it stays Daddy's little secret.

Unfortunately, all the other reading I do during the day is less easy to hide. Any magazines that come in the mail after lunch need to be read immediately, before the information gets stale, even the next week's *TV Guide*. I read them with care because Lora can detect a dog-eared *Rolling Stone* or *Sports Illustrated,* especially one with pieces of Fruity Pebbles stuck in the pages. Cotton mittens are not a bad idea.

As a freelance writer, I'm lucky to have my laptop computer – it's a great excuse. I keep it with me all the time. If Lora calls and asks what I'm doing, I simply set the Victoria's Secret catalog to the side and tap on the keys of the computer.

"I'm typing away here, hon, can't you hear it?"

"You're not playing computer games, are you, Joe?"

(Make sure the sound control on the computer is turned down, or the "Wheel of Fortune" theme song will bust you every time.)

I finally learned to tell Lora, "Don't call during naptime." I just didn't add "particularly mine."

Of course, all of the magazine reading, couch laying, and TV watching are things Lora suspects, but she just doesn't need to *know* them. No matter what I keep from her, however, the loving Lora wants to be home, so it's important to remind her of how tough the duty really is.

So when Seth wakes up earlier than usual and is a little bear all morning, I tell Lora:

"He screamed when I changed him and yelled when I fed him breakfast. He cried when I turned the TV on, and he cried louder when I turned it off. There was nothing that I could do to please him – he even threw a tantrum when I gave him the cookies he whined for."

And what about dinnertime? At five o'clock, I'm usually racing to get dinner finished, wash yesterday's dishes, and pick up the mess I had promised to clean up at noon – all in the final fifteen minutes before Lora is expected. Just then, Seth, impatient for his dinner, attaches himself to my pant leg, dragging himself around the kitchen after me and whining for a snack. Why would any sane person want to handle those stressful moments?

When Lora walks in the door, Seth's mood usually changes (at least for the moment). The working mother gets her reward as Seth runs across the room and throws himself in her arms with triumphant cheers and hugs. Mommy is the queen, and Daddy is the evil ogre who wouldn't give him a snack.

Sometimes, a kid just needs his mother, and there's nothing his dad can do about it. And that's something the working mother *really* doesn't need to know.

Another thing that doesn't always have to be passed on is the difference in discipline depending on who's around. When you're with a child all day and just can't bear to hear the fortieth request for Cheetos, it's easier to give in when Big Mother is not watching. You can always toe the line later in the day when there is a fresh defense on hand to help.

On the other hand, a househusband with an audience of none has the opportunity for a little extra discipline where he sees fit, without consulting the spouse who might have a different opinion. Take, for example, the adventure of Seth's pacifier.

Lora and I were in slight disagreement on what to do about Seth's pacifier as he approached his second birthday. Lora thought Seth would lose it on his own when he was ready, and I simply hated it. I wanted it out of his mouth for good, and I thought he needed a little push to do it.

Let me clarify first of all that Seth was the original "nukie" prince. He had five different nukies, which Lora bought during his first months, in the new parent's fear that we would lose them and be unable to put him to sleep. As a result, over those first two years, he grew to require all five nukies in order to go to sleep. He would lay in his bed and cry out "nuk" until he had all five of them clutched by the nipples in his little fists. Then he would taste each of them until he had decided on the flavor for the evening.

Even Lora felt that this was kind of excessive.

I decided that if I did nothing else while I was home with my son, I would certainly rid him of this pariah. I feared that my kid would be smoking in the second grade if we didn't get these sucking machines out of his mouth – immediately. So I made it my personal mission to destroy the nukie habit, a clandestine propaganda campaign that happened whenever Lora wasn't around.

Figuring that Seth couldn't count, I started by "losing" nukies, one at a time. The first one to go was one that Seth always complained tasted "icky" – he didn't mind holding it when he slept, but he didn't want it in his mouth. I put it up high in a cupboard, where Seth (and Lora) would never find it.

At naptime that day, I gave Seth the four nukies and waited.

"Nukie!" Seth demanded.

"I don't know, Seth," I said, making an elaborate search around the room. "I can't find it. Nukie gone."

Maybe because this was the icky nukie, Seth accepted it pretty well. Using this technique, over time, I whittled his use down to only one nukie, and that one only for sleeping. Yet I wanted to go all the way.

It finally happened one afternoon before his nap. I finished reading Seth books in his bed, and then he spotted the one remaining pacifier under the covers.

"You don't need that nukie, Seth," I intoned, my usual mantra. "Why don't we throw it away?"

I expected the usual whine of "My nukie!" Instead, I heard "Yeah, icky nukie – throw away."

Stunned, I asked him again, and he repeated it. I scrambled to my feet, reinforcing the idea over and over, each time describing that terrible nukie in increasingly disgusting detail.

"Yeah, let's get rid of that yucky, blecchy nukie."

Amazingly, Seth agreed with me. I hurried into our bedroom, where the closest wastebasket could be found. Spotting some tissues, I placed a layer of them on the bottom of the wastebasket, thinking that this little scenario might not last. Seth was bound to get sucker's remorse and change his mind.

He walked into the bedroom, looked down at the cavernous wastebasket, and at one final urging from dad, dropped the nukie in. I congratulated him with a hug and a kiss, hustled him off to his bedroom, and settled him in for his nap.

After I left his room, I retrieved the pacifier and tissues (to erase any trace of the incident) and then got on the phone to Lora. Of course, my triumphant crowing left out some of the details. I made it sound like Seth did it all on his own – I didn't mention the encouragement from Seth's nuk-independence counselor.

"He'll be looking for it when he gets up from his nap," Lora warned, somewhat jealously, I thought.

When Seth woke up, he responded right on cue by asking for his nukie. I reminded him of what he'd done and added that I had put it in the garbage can outside.

"Daddy get nukie," he said.

"We can't," I improvised. "The garbage guys took it away."

As a diversion, I took him outside. We played for a while and had just sat down to rest when Seth brought up the nukie again. I retold the tale, struggling to describe just what condition the pacifier was now in. Suddenly, looking across the yard, I noticed a garbage truck moving up the street. I pointed it out to Seth.

"Garbage guys took nukie," I said, successfully allaying the blame, but feeling a bit like Richard Nixon blaming the plumbers for the Watergate break-in.

Seth bought it. Every once in a while since then, though, he'll look at me and out of the blue say, "Garbage guys take nukie."

After Seth had forgotten about the pacifier, I filled Lora in on the details of my own involvement. And while Lora is happy that the pacifier is gone, she probably would have taken a different approach. I look back on my little ruse with pride, a feather in my househusband's cap.

Had I conferred with the working mom before implementing my plan, Seth might still be sucking on a pacifier. Sitting at work confronted only with images of Seth sans nukie, not with the real thing, she couldn't endure the discomfort of imagining his pain in losing his security. Perhaps, as long as Seth acts like mommy's baby, he remains her baby, unchanged while she is away.

I can understand that mentality. But I had to look at the kid with his plug in everyday, so I couldn't stand the reality. I had to do something about it.

It made me feel like I had passed a milestone in my house-husbandry journey. I took parenting matters into my own hand without first consulting the All-Knowing Mother and succeeded in accomplishing my goal – a goal we both wanted, even though the means might have been different. For once, I felt confident enough to say, "I'm here with this kid all day, I know what's going on, and this is what needs to be done." Any mother would have done the same.

I've even begun plotting a course for potty training – still flush (pun intended) with the thrill of my victory.

It may be a short-lived one, however. Lora has brought home some literature on video-phones – in an attempt to increase her motherly surveillance. Can the working mom coming home be far behind?

Chapter 20
Iron Joe

Back before I became a househusband, a friend and fellow parent suggested that I read Robert Bly's book *Iron John*. Credited with fueling the men's movement, this book uses an old fairy tale to illustrate, in part, how fathers need to be involved in raising their sons and how modern society has shunted the father's responsibilities aside. At the time, I thought that if my son merely refrains from killing me and sleeping with my wife, I'll be doing a fine job as a father.

But since I acquired my new station in life, I've decided to give *Iron John* a read. I'll admit that I worry whether the sight of his old man in an apron is going to confuse Seth's search for a role model long before the closeness we've built up ever clears it up. What's he going to want to learn from me – cleaning tips?

I'm halfway through the book now, and let me say that I haven't felt compelled to join any all-male half-naked romps through the forest, beating my chest like a bass drum and howling as if I've just run through a thorn bush without a loin cloth. That part of the men's movement sounds more fun to read about than actually experience.

Still, reading Bly's ruminations on manhood has been beneficial – even though I've done it with dishpan hands. At the very least, it's raised my consciousness about the importance of fatherhood and made me feel virtuous about the time I'm spending with my son. After all, if the bad old industrial life of the 1950s, with fathers trudging off to the factories at five a.m. every day, destroyed the connection between father and son, then Seth and I sleeping in until nine a.m. most days must be doing something to restore it.

But one of Bly's main points, I think, is worth pondering for all parents. If a father works so hard that he has no energy left at the end of the day to teach his children anything, then something important has been lost. Maybe one of those special things a father can do is pass on what he's learned in life.

I personally am looking forward to sharing my love of the outdoors with my son. (My wife, who knows me as a sprawled-in-front-of-the-TV sort of guy, doesn't believe this.) But much of my young adulthood was spent in the woods, hiking, skiing, camping, cooking over an open fire – okay, drinking a couple beers – and just generally feeling alive. I want my son to know that exciting feeling of vulnerability at being away from home and that confidence that can be earned only from mastering the wilds of nature. It seems worthwhile to pass on to my son the knowledge of building a fire outdoors – he's already mastered the art of warming up a television and putting another tape in the VCR.

Still, hiking is only a recreation, and Bly's advice goes much deeper, into the heart of day-to-day living. I'm not advocating a return to Bly's fabled tribal way of life, when fathers initiated their sons into manhood by plucking them from their mothers' arms and exposing them to the dangers of hunting and gathering. But maybe fathers should teach their sons skills that are today's equivalents, to help them survive everyday life in the twenty-first century.

Take me, for example. I'm a writer. If I hunt and gather anything to survive, it's words. I hunt them in my brain, capture them from books, pluck them from conversations, and then gather them on the computer screen. Unfortunately, about the only time I can go on these forays into the intellectual jungle is when Seth is taking his afternoon nap. When he does find me typing, it usually becomes a battle of wills that results in my surrendering the keyboard and him typing alphabet soup while the computer beeps warning sounds. This lasts until I fear for the computer's life and drag Seth kicking and screaming from the room. And then what have I passed on besides my short temper and the fact that I'm stronger than my two-year-old son? Probably nothing.

As a househusband, I certainly have the time to make an important impression on Seth. And I know that I have the desire to teach him what I know about life. It's just that passing on writing skills is more difficult than showing your son how to harvest a crop. While there are similarities – manure is spread abundantly in both professions – the restrictive clause comma rule doesn't hold a toddler's attention like playing in the dirt.

Thinking about what I can teach Seth has also made me think about my own father. How can I know what to pass on to my son until I'm sure of what's been passed on to me?

First off, my dad did teach me the gathering part of "hunting and gathering." Having grown up on a farm, he kept his hand in with a garden in our backyard and another at the family farm (still run by his brother). I spent springs planting potatoes, summers pulling weeds in the soybean fields, and falls plucking chickens. Unfortunately, it only taught me that I didn't want to farm the rest of my life.

The same goes for being a plumber, which my dad did for twenty-five years. He worked on a construction crew at a soybean refinery, and the smell when he came home from work was enough to convince me that plumbing was not the job for me. Yet, ironically enough, I worked at that same plant during the summer before I went to college. By this time, Dad was a union business agent, and he had gotten me this job as a construction laborer. On my first day, he gave me a ride home from work and smelled that old familiar smell on me – his smile told me that plumbing wasn't his life's work either.

Even though my dad wasn't my labor mentor, I don't think that the "father angst" described in *Iron John* really applies to me. True, my dad went to work every morning at the factory, but at nights and on weekends he taught me how to fish, garden, and play baseball. When he wasn't showing me how to throw a fastball, he was painting a batter's strike zone on the garage or building nets for our backyard hockey rink. He was there when he could be, and he always seemed to be having a good time.

I talked with my dad this morning, about the old days and what I'm going through now as a dad. He admits that he missed out on some things because of his job. But he also said that he treasures the memories of spending time with us on the ball diamond, in the back yard, at football games, fishing, and at my uncle's farm.

And maybe this is what Bly is really writing about. It's more than teaching any particular skills or passing on a choice of professions. What a father really needs to do is be physically, spiritually, and emotionally present for his son.

My dad and I have that kind of relationship – we're pretty good friends – and I hope that someday Seth and I will be able to take the same feelings away from our experiences together. Even though I wonder what effect my househusband role will have on my son, I'll always feel good about the connection that I've made with him during our time together.

Maybe I'll get out the old manual typewriter for Seth to bang on tonight. And when he's done, I'll see if he'd like me to read an extra book to him before he goes to sleep. Maybe even something I've written.

Part V
Summer Again

Daddy's gone back to work – be home after the game.

Epilogue: Birth of the Sequel

As I write this, it's July 14, two years after I first came home to be a househusband, and the last day of my freedom. Tomorrow, I go back to work. I should be excited – and tomorrow I may be – but today I feel nothing but a palpable sense of loss and depression.

For the past two years, I've had the privilege of living in my son's world full-time. I've seen Seth grow from an inarticulate and stumbling toddler into a small boy with boundless energy and enthusiasm and a joyous curiosity toward life. We've shared hugs, laughter, more cartoons than I ever thought I'd watch, endless car games, and hundreds of little daytime adventures. This is an opportunity that many mothers – and the vast majority of fathers – never have.

And now it's coming to an end.

When I quit work two years ago, I seriously wondered if I'd ever be employed again. I was afraid no one would want an unemployed, almost-fortysomething male with a huge gap in his resume. But then I was offered a job editing publications for Minnesota's NBA basketball franchise. What red-blooded American male could refuse a job with a professional sports team? I think of it as my reward for changing thousands of dirty diapers.

I should be anticipating finally going back to work. But

I'm not. In March, Lora gave birth to our second child, a beautiful little girl named Tessa Marie – and once again, our whole world is created anew. Lora and I were both home for the first three months of Tessa's life (thanks to a generous maternity leave from Lora's company), and that helped to ease our transition into a two-child family.

But at the same time, once Lora was spending all day at home, the jig for me was basically up. Any fun I had had as a househusband came to a screeching halt as I chased around the house tending to the demands of one postpartum mother, one new baby, and one formerly only child. Late-night TV, sleeping in, and afternoon naps all quickly became a thing of the past. It was about this time that I had my first serious thoughts about finding a new job.

Tessa had a big hand in this process. She's a great kid, with big, beautiful brown eyes and a quiet, solemn demeanor, but she takes in every little trick her older brother plays on me, and she's come up with a whole array of needs that Seth never dreamed of. It wasn't long after Lora went back to work that she and Seth provided me with days of tag-team crying, afternoons of alternating naps, and the understanding of what it's like to run in a vat of molasses – you keep going all day, but you never get anywhere.

On the other hand, Tessa has also blessed me with an intimate acquaintance with many facets of babyhood that I wasn't home to enjoy with Seth. I've watched her learn how to smile and then laugh, I've marveled at her ability to fold herself in half to get her toes into her mouth, and I've learned how to clean rice cereal out of every piece of clothing in the house. Her obvious and genuine love for me has made it easier to take regurgitated formula stains on my favorite Timberwolves sweatshirt.

Still, with two children, I knew it was only a matter of time before I was done. Lora is quitting her job and will be coming home to stay with the kids, so I know they will be in good hands. But that's not what's bothering me at the moment.

Over time, I've seen Seth pull away, ever so slowly, from my tutelage and start to adventure out on his own. I've felt both pride and sadness at his growing independence of me. While his growth signals, in a small way, that I've done my job well, I can't help but wonder if he'll forget how close we've been once I'm no longer a twenty-four-hour-a-day presence in his life.

What will Seth take away from this now-too-short experience? Will Lora hear a litany of "Daddy let me do that," "Daddy doesn't do it that way," and "I miss my Daddy" or will it be "Daddy always yelled at me"? I know I taught him how to work the VCR, but what of lasting value have I given him?

Most important, will he remember that I was here at all? Will he someday be proud to say, "My dad stayed home to take care of me"? Or will he remember all too well and someday wonder what was wrong with me? My only consolation is that, whatever example I've set, it doesn't stop with my going back to work – for an employed father, the work of child care goes on at night and every weekend.

Seth has changed so much even since I wrote the last chapter of this diary. Much of what was difficult and painful or awkward and funny when I first came home is now history, a stepping stone – whether I want it to be or not – to where Seth is today. Lora and I are forever changed, as well. As a result of our experiences, we have a greater respect for each other and a greater awareness of how the role a person plays in the family affects their behavior: whenever a wife complains that her husband just wants to sit back and read the paper when he comes home at night, we smile because Lora wanted to do the same thing and we recognize the working person's exhaustion that's behind it.

When I look back at this diary, I'm amazed at where we are today. The time seems to have raced, like one of Seth's cars, to this point. As I read some of the passages and then look at my son, I am happy and proud of who he is, but other sections have me cringing, wondering exactly who that was who tried to put out a kitchen oil fire with a towel.

With Tessa fast approaching this same stage, a quick review of Seth's most recent progress can't hurt. To paraphrase an old adage: "Those who don't remember past parenting tactics are doomed!!!"

Seth transposed our names for a long time, referring to us as Mahdaddy and Damommy. This effect of our role reversal seems to be permanent – now that he's learned to talk better, it's metamorphosed into "my dear mommy" and "my dear daddy." Everyone thinks it's cute, but Lora and I know it's because he couldn't figure out what to call us when he was learning to talk.

Seth also reached the pinnacle of using one parent against the other: Upon being scolded by his mother, Seth said, "Only daddy take care of kids." When Lora told me about it, I feared the end of the world as I knew it. But Lora didn't even respond. She merely reported the facts and walked away. Even the ultra-paranoid Lora adjusted to our role change, in the end.

When we go to church now, Seth is bored with Cheerios, so we've started bringing cars to keep him occupied. But he's an observant child. He's watched us go to communion enough times that he has his eye on a different kind of church-time snacking: "I go get marshmallows from my Jesus," Seth said, referring to the priest. "And then I go sit in the chairs." I guess we're going to have to start bringing Lucky Charms to church.

Band-Aids are now the cure-all for everything in our house. They can help everything from Seth's scraped knee to Grover's missing fur – no healing househusband should be without them. The only thing with more uses is duct tape.

As far as the TV wars go, television is now ahead by two at our house: we now have a big-screen TV and the Cartoon Network. The big-screen TV was a gift – honest to God! – a used one from my father-in-law, but I didn't say no to it. How could any sports fan turn down thirty-five inches of NFL action? But the Cartoon Network is Lora's fault. It certainly puts a lie to one of the easiest excuses for turning the TV off: "Sorry, Seth, there's no more cartoons on anymore." He knows better.

Unfortunately, with all this artillery on its side, television has claimed another victim in our family. Tessa is shaping up to be just as big a video-head as her brother.

Haircuts have never been a problem since the time I cut Seth's hair myself. The next time his haircut rolled around, I asked Seth whether he wanted Daddy or the lady at the hair salon to cut it. Three times I asked that question, and three times he replied, without equivocation, "The lady." Sheesh, he must be scared of a little blood.

A summer of drought has returned my lawn to its rightful condition: patchy, pockmarked, and a jaundiced yellow. It goes well with the dandelions, however. This summer, I went ahead with my plan for organic lawncare and loaded down the grass with some nitrogen enriched fertilizer. Unfortunately, I didn't pay attention to the amount recommended to spread on the lawn – and I piled it on. High concentration killed every blade of grass in the test area. The worst part is, I thought I was making each pass of the spreader right next to the previous one, but I wasn't. My backyard now looks like it has crop circles made by drunken extra-terrestrials.

Seth occasionally says he has work to do and practices banging out letters on the computer. This makes me feel like I've made an impression on him, but Lora wishes I'd pass on a career that makes money.

Yet I am employed now, and for me, remembering the diapers, tantrums, and battles will help ease the pain of separation while I'm at work. (They make for better office conversation, as well.) But I know that's not what I'll dwell on. The pictures I hang on my cubicle wall will be smiling ones and so will my memories.

I came home to take care of my son, and I feel good about it. My presence made a difference, I believe. While it's possible that the instability of Lora and me changing roles may have screwed up my kid, I don't think so. Giving a child all of your love, time, and attention can't hurt.

I'm not so naive to think that having a parent stay home to raise my children will be a cure-all and we will live happily ever after. I know that Seth and Tessa will have problems growing up, just like every kid has. And I also know that everything

Lora and I do – or don't do – in raising them from here on out will also have its impact on the rest of their lives. The best thing about it is that *we* will be the ones having the impact – that was the reason for our choice.

I've received a tremendous gift the past two years. The time I spent with Seth – and then Tessa – can never be matched in my lifetime. So I shouldn't feel sad at the loss of my house-husband lifestyle because it would be lamenting a gift I might not normally have had – and was very lucky to get. I am already ahead of the game in this category of life experiences when compared with my dad.

Somewhere within these pages is a gift back to my children. Someday, I hope they will read this book with affection – first, for learning things about their childhood that I might not have remembered to tell them, and second, for recognizing the love and sacrifices that Lora and I both made to raise them at home. That is the real gift, manifested in this book, that we are giving back to our children.

When this diary is published, I fully expect someone to ask me, "Well, you took care of your kids. So what? What's so special about that? What makes you different from me or any other parent before you that you should write a book?"

My answer will be, "Nothing. But you should have written one. It's so special an opportunity that you should have something to remember it the rest of your life."

About the Author

Besides his stint as a househusband, Joseph Oberle has been a feature writer and St. Paul city editor for *Skyway News,* a weekly newspaper in the Twin Cities of Minneapolis and St. Paul, and a staff editor at *Training* magazine, a national trade publication. His freelance articles have appeared in a variety of newspapers and magazines.

Currently, Joseph is publications manager for the Minnesota Timberwolves NBA basketball team. *Diary of a Mad Househusband* is his second book. The first, titled *Anchorage,* is an educational book for children about that Alaska city.

Joseph and his wife, Lora, live in Fridley, Minnesota, with their children, Seth, Tessa, and Paige Lee, who was born during the production of this book.